Pension Matters

Your guide through the retirement income maze

Pension Matters

First published in 2011 by

Ecademy Press

48 St Vincent Drive, St Albans, Hertfordshire, AL1 5SJ

info@ecademy-press.com www.ecademy-press.com

Printed and Bound by Lightning Source in the UK and USA

Set by Charlotte Mouncey

Printed on acid-free paper from managed forests.
This book is printed on demand, so no copies will be remaindered or pulped.

ISBN 978-1-905823-96-3

A CIP catalogue record for this book is available from the British Library.

Acknowledgements

A big and heartfelt thank you to Jackie for her unwavering support without which nothing would ever get completed. My thanks to Mindy Gibbins-Klein whose attentive midwifery ensured this book was born without complication and the staff at Ecademy Press for their saintly patience. Gratitude is also extended to Geoff Stenton and Neil Todd, Accountants of probity who took the time out to read the very rough first draft and offer suitable words of encouragement. Applause to Mark Bryant for his creative input and not least thanks to Ian Dicks of the Financial Times for the cartoons, who says Pensions can't be fun!

Foreword

The intention of this book is to provide you and all those thinking about their Pensions with the opportunity to experience a more fulfilling and meaningful retirement. No longer are people sleepwalking into retirement in a state of supine acceptance, the fact that you have picked up this book is yet further evidence of that. The quality of your life when you cease work is largely determined by your ability to make sound financial choices and the more secure you are financially the broader the spectrum of choice will be. The quality of your decisions will certainly be enhanced if they are flavoured with a clarity of understanding and coloured by an awareness of what your Pension income options truly are.

Knowledge and information are essential but are no substitute for experience and professional advice. This book seeks to bring together all of those factors by examining some of the key concepts, income and investment strategies that are available to you, whether you are already retired or just beginning to give the issue serious thought. There are a spiralling number of retirement income innovations and we examine an assortment of them in the coming chapters to provide you with an appreciation of how the various methods can be applied for your personal benefit. Should you glean just one small idea from this book that enriches your financial situation over the years ahead then my efforts will have been justified, as I hope will your investment in this book.

Contents

1 When tomorrow becomes today

Why you really need to read this book

In the year 1900 Queen Victoria was not amused for a number of reasons, not least by having to give up some time in her own leisurely retirement to send 100 telegrams. Dispatched to all corners of the Empire upon which the sun never set, this new form of high-speed communication was greeted with wonderment by those of her subjects who, despite the rigors of the workhouse, colonial wars, poverty and disease had been fortunate enough to live to celebrate their 100th birthday.

Amused or not, Queen Vic didn't know how lucky she was compared to her great granddaughter Queen Elizabeth II. In the year 2006, little more than 100 years later, which in evolutionary terms is less than a cosmic heartbeat, the number of centenary telegrams being dispatched from Buckingham Palace had multiplied to a staggering 6,000, a figure predicted to rise to a postbag bursting 95,000 a year by the year 2060.

So what has this got to do with my retirement? The short answer is everything. In our humble telegram statistic lays the single most critical factor affecting Pension planning in the developed world – longevity and its ever-increasing demands on Pensions and savings. Regardless of whether you are 18 or 80 it will have, if it hasn't already, an impact on your income in your post-work years. The wealthier you are, of course, the less you will be affected but be assured, affected you will be.

Longevity is a word that may rarely enter your vocabulary but it is going to be playing a part in your life, not only by placing a bigger strain on your income, it will be increasing your taxes, restricting availability to healthcare, and placing ever greater pressure on natural resources. The cost of our collective presence beyond our allotted three score years and 10 is going to impact on every aspect of your life, large and small.

I am focusing on the impact this will have upon residents of the British Isles generally and you in particular. I can see no point in adding to the growing sense of unease by looking at the worldwide consequences of longevity as an escalating global population (estimated to rise by another 2 billion to 8 billion over the next 40 years) pursue scarce resources driving up the cost of food, power, even fresh water will become an increasingly valuable commodity as the number of people washing their smalls worldwide grows by another 12,000 every single day.

Governments are faced with very difficult choices, the most difficult one being 'which option is most likely to get me re-elected?' Pensions in the UK are a little like daytime television, you think that whatever anyone does it couldn't possibly get any worse and then it does. Unfortunately in the Pensions arena there are no real vote winners and it is the political wilderness for any aspiring politician, just witness the ten different ministers with responsibility for Pensions we had during 13 years of Labour government.

Put simply, either we all continue to work ever longer with the State Pension Age getting harder in the distance to see, and that's not just as a result of your failing eyesight, or we are forced to pay more during our working lives. More than likely it will be a combination of the two so it is vital that the choices you make at retirement are the right ones as it is hard to see any genuine improvement in what Governments of any hue have to offer us in terms of retirement income.

The Government appears to believe that if they make the raising of the State Pension Age far enough in the future and gently bring it back towards the present it somehow won't seem so painful. We were looking at the raising of State Pension Age to 66 in 2023; that has now travelled back through time to become 2020 with a further rise planned to age 68. Postponing state retirement age to 70 is now a real possibility and as the gravity of the UK's financial situation becomes more apparent you can be sure this figure will gradually be dragged closer to the present in the coming years.

More years added to your life sentence, no time off for good taxpaying behaviour, but it doesn't even begin to solve the problem. We could, of course, reduce the State Pension and associated means-tested benefits but again this is something that could not happen overnight, it would probably take a couple of decades to wash it through the benefit system, and once again it is not a plan that is guaranteed to return your local Honourable Member to Westminster with a comfortable majority.

Not only is it political suicide to attack the benefits of the elderly, who are the fastest-growing segment of the voting population, there is something morally repugnant about taking away from those more vulnerable members of society, especially when they have worked all their lives under the misapprehension that the State will take care of them, however modestly, in their dotage.

This, of course, is conjoined with ever-rising taxes to subsidise those who have never saved a bean during their working lives and now expect the State (that's you and me by the way) to support them in their twilight years, and being a civilized nation of course we will do, maybe through gritted teeth but we do it all the same.

So that's the conundrum the Government has to work through, but what about us? What can we do to help ease the financial pain that awaits us after a lifetime of sweat and taxes? Everybody knows we need to save more, and we need to invest what we save more wisely. That's where we come in; hopefully this book will lift the fog from your retirement landscape in respect of the options open to you and provide some clear guidance as to how you can get the most from your retirement funds.

For the over 50s, retirement plays an escalating part in the financial thought process so I am going to focus on the choices available as you approach retirement to maximize your retirement income and protect yourself as far as possible from the vagaries of Government policy, worldwide economics and the colourful individuals that populate the murky world of grand finance.

The fact that you have picked up this book proves you are serious about your retirement planning and that deserves a pat on the back to start with; so many people are happy to drift along on the tide of life being buffeted by economic crises and Government policy and then moan they have not got the retirement they dreamed off. Worse are those that make a definite decision that they are not going to make any effort at all and then have the audacity to moan that their lifestyle is not commensurate with the fantasy retirement they have been dreaming of – there is not a palm tree in sight and the only time they enjoy getting some heat is when they are flush enough to put the gas fire on.

Compound these issues with the severe financial crisis of 2008/09 that has left Government accounts – not to mention Pension funds – looking severely battered and we have a recipe for bread and gruel on which to sustain us during our later years. Pension schemes are closing faster than you can say 'final salary', returns from insurance Company funds remain uncertain and the complexity of the Pension and tax system challenges even the finest minds, so where do we go from here?

The purpose of this book is not to provide answers to the world's Pension problems – there are many brilliant minds perpetually engaged in that task. The purpose of this book is to provide answers to YOUR Pension problems, some simple strategies and solutions to the problems you and your income are facing in retirement. Pensions come with a plethora of questions but very few right or wrong answers and only time will tell if the decisions you made were the right ones. Yet, furnished with the right information, advice and an understanding sufficient to make those decisions, it can provide you with the optimum if not necessarily the ideal solution. These decisions have to be made with insufficient time and money against a background of uncertainty and a complex array of tax law mixed with ever increasing choices and investment innovation.

As youthful dreams evolve into middle-age reality, aspirations for retirement can change dramatically. Fate doesn't necessarily reward those who are prudent, with random injustice in the form of redundancy, divorce, failing business, dependent children (are they ever anything else?) or even elderly relatives. The jar we keep attempting to fill marked 'retirement' keeps being turned upside down and emptied by life, it never quite gets refilled to the level we not only desire but know we should have. That round-the-world sailing adventure, trip to Peru, or even a steady 10 days winter warmth on the Costas can look progressively unlikely as retirement beckons. With this book to assist you the chances of making the correct decisions about your income in retirement will undoubtedly be improved and you can look to the future with greater confidence, sitting if not in luxury then at least in comfort, patiently awaiting that telegram from Buckingham Palace.

2 What you really, really want

Clarify your priorities

How long is retirement?

"Retirement is a 52 week a year holiday!" or so my uncle used to say. In reality it's much longer than that. With a holiday you have a start date and an end date so you can budget your time and money accordingly. Retirement certainly has an end date but we don't know when that is and the longer we envisage it is going to be the more challenging it is to allocate our limited resources to it. No matter where in the world you live, or how fortunate you have been in the genetic lottery of evolution, the number of days ahead of you, especially those in good health, are incalculable.

We can, of course, make an educated guess: an average man retiring at age 65 today can expect to live for another 17 years, a woman for almost 20, so by definition you have a 50% chance of passing that average milestone, but how many of those years will be in good health and how many of us are average anyway? If there are two of you the situation becomes doubly complicated, and these are mysteries that apply to us all regardless of circumstance. So if we can't budget for our time or our health we can certainly have a good go at budgeting for our finances to make sure we get the most out of the rest of our lives, be it 1 year or 40 years. If it was only one year it would be easy of course, but we need to budget for 40, just in case.

Unless you are fabulously wealthy, (and if you are you don't need to spend time reading this book, go and do something useful like beat the servants) then you have to use your limited financial resources to serve you as best as possible over the longer term and the more limited those resources, the more important those budgetary decisions are. We are seeking what economists call the 'optimum allocation of resources' which involves you making some difficult choices and this chapter is designed to provide you with some of the tools you will need for the job. The choices you make at retirement will affect the rest of your life; this is the first step in assisting you in making the right ones.

Even with the most highly polished crystal ball it is impossible for us to make accurate financial forecasts, but retirement, like all other aspects of life, is a journey, and if your destination is a land of peace, free from financial worry then this chapter helps you make the first step on that voyage of discovery. Like any journey you must first establish exactly where you are today before you can even begin heading in the right direction.

Before considering your priorities, which should be the scenic highlights of your journey, you need to consider the essentials you will need to prepare, to be certain you are exactly where you think you are financially before you begin even thinking about that first step into retirement. This is the easy part; you probably have a pretty good idea where you are financially as I am sure you have been thinking about this for some time, with your mind becoming increasingly focused on retirement as the years pass and the momentous day approaches.

Me plc

You are going to undertake a rigorous audit of your financial self. It can be exciting, it can be frightening and perhaps even a little depressing, but it needs to be done because without this the rest of your plans are meaningless. If you don't have a plan you are living your life by accident.

If you think of yourself as a business this exercise is the drawing up of accounts for 'me plc' and the first stage is to complete your own personal Balance Sheet. This will provide you with an overview of the whole of your financial life to date. There are numerous spreadsheets you can use for this exercise, you can download all sorts of freebies from www.office.microsoft.com/templates or design your own on Excel if you prefer. Alternatively a simple sheet of paper will serve you just as well. A line straight down the middle to create two columns, the left entitled Assets (what you own) and the right entitled Liabilities (what you owe). Start adding things and their value as they come to mind. For example the first thing in the Assets column may be, House £200,000 and in the corresponding right hand column Mortgage £42,000 and so on.

Examples of things appearing in the left hand side can include items that are tangible and easy to value such as Cash, ISAs, Investment Bonds, National Savings Certificates and of course Pension Funds. Get up-to-date values and establish if these are guaranteed or subject to change, for example your stocks and shares ISA might be changing in value every day. Towards the bottom half of the page, begin to add items that are less easy to value such as your car, jewellery, antiques and so on.

The liabilities column should include all outstanding and ongoing debts such as credit cards, loans, car finance etc. My hope is that your left hand column will have a figure at the bottom in excess of that at the bottom of the right hand side of the page. If this is not the case, don't worry you are far from alone, and there are steps we can take to help, but more of that later.

We want to eliminate as much as possible from the right hand column before we begin our retirement journey even if this means sacrificing some of our capital forever because I am fairly certain that a bit further through this chapter when I ask you to list your priorities, 'financial security' will be near the top end of your hit parade and reducing debt is a huge step towards achieving that very worthwhile goal.

No debt no danger

How much you have in your right hand column will depend on your attitude and outlook on life, if you have the view of the current retired generation that equates debt with the never-never, on tick and the workhouse, you will probably have very little or any debt as you approach retirement. If, on the other hand, you feel very much a part of the baby boomer generation that embraced consumerism and debt in all its forms you may have an array of items in your liabilities column, many of which we are going to seek to eliminate.

Remortgaging our homes has become the simplest and cheapest way to access additional capital and keep increasing our levels of debt throughout our working lives. Spending money we haven't got is a habit and building up loans and credit cards has become a national pastime fuelled by ever-increasing house prices. Even the so-called 'credit crunch' may have only temporarily applied the brakes to a vehicle that has long since been charging downhill out of control and heading for a crash. The worldwide financial crisis is the culmination of millions of personal crises, and you may be one of them, but this doesn't mean there isn't a solution.

Mortgage Brokers know that, despite the good intentions of those remortgaging 'just this once' to get themselves back on an even keel, the vast majority will be back in a couple of years to repeat the exercise and add another £20k or £50k to their mortgage with the view that one day they are going to start paying it off. Sadly for the vast majority that 'one day', like tomorrow, never comes. When retirement arrives this unpleasant financial reality has to be addressed as your income will almost certainly reduce, servicing your existing debt will be harder and obtaining further credit very difficult if not impossible.

Store cards and credit cards should be eliminated as far as possible, starting with the highest charging ones first, loans paid off or restructured and car loans avoided at all costs. Never borrow money to pay for a depreciating asset and a car is the best and worst example of that.

Which items cannot be paid off at the outset of your retirement? Be ruthless, what do you really need? When we get to the 'me plc' Profit and Loss Account further along we can look at establishing a plan to pay off all debts within a reasonable time. There will inevitably be exceptions, and yes I know there are people that will say they are quite happy to leave their buy-to-let flat run indefinitely on 'interest only' but to me this still carries dangers, what if interest rates rise dramatically and your mortgage is substantially higher than your rental income? Or you cannot rent out your property for long periods?

More than 50% of over 65s owe significant amounts of money with the average being £36,000, the over 70s owe an average of £41,000, more than £9,000 of that on credit cards alone. To quote Dean Mirfion of Key Retirement Solutions "Servicing debt cannot continue to be a way of life once you no longer have an income to comfortably make repayments." I couldn't put it more succinctly myself.

Income-producing assets

Begin to consider which assets are sources of income, the Pension plans are obvious, but is it time to start withdrawing income from your ISAs or releasing capital from your home to provide an income? There are, of course, some assets that realistically you can disregard as potential sources of income, you might be happy to sell that old Picasso hanging above the fireplace, but the wife's jewellery, it's not going to happen is it?

We need to take a very stern look at the 'Me plc' Balance Sheet as it is the culmination of a lifetime's work, and let's not make any assumptions about house prices going up 10% a year or Investment Bonds growing at 15% every year, far safer to take the conservative view. A strong dose of realism is what's needed to arrive at a single, simple figure, ideally a pound sign followed by a number with several zeros after it, but if that is not the case some serious prioritizing needs to be done. If you are facing retirement with a seemingly insurmountable hill of debts, there are solutions, and you may take some comfort that you are in the underfunded majority.

Me plc – Profit and Loss

One of the principal changes at retirement is that you will no longer be receiving a monthly payment from your employer or your business and will have to examine your budget accordingly. The second part of the 'Me plc' exercise is your personal Profit and Loss Account, essentially your income and expenditure, a budget as accurately as you can be in respect of your ongoing living expenses.

Once again we simply need a sheet of paper divided into two columns (or download a template), left hand column reads 'income' right hand 'expenditure' and away we go. The left hand will include State Pension and any Social Security benefits to which you may be entitled, Company Pensions, Income Bonds, bank interest, dividends, rental income, ISA income and the like. The right hand column is more difficult. As you are entering a whole new way of living your expenses are going to change (remember that 52 week holiday?), you will no longer have to pay to travel to work but you will be in the house twice as much so your heating bills are going to be higher.

Once again we are seeking a figure in the right hand column that is smaller than the figure on the left. If this is not the case there needs to be some serious scratching of heads as to what actually is a necessity and what could reasonably be assumed to fall into the 'luxuries' category. It is important that we balance the books at outset otherwise your financial retirement strategy will simply not be sustainable.

We need to split each column into two horizontally and divide it into 'fixed' and 'variable' costs. Fixed are those items that have to be paid, necessities (for the record, golf club membership is not considered a necessity), Council Tax, utilities, telephone, food, clothes and so forth. Variables, what we could describe as discretionary expenses, will be holidays, meals out, new furniture, decorating and gardening expenses.

It is the variables that require prioritizing and inevitably there will be some compromises along the way. Is changing the car more important than an extra holiday? Depends on your point of view but agreement needs to be reached, even if it is by the toss of a coin!

There will be enough unforseens along the way to challenge your assumptions so it is important that we have a sound base to work from. Very often the difficulty is in establishing what is a realistic income you could expect from your Pension funds? What options are there to protect it? Will it increase? What happens to my income for my Spouse if I die first? There are numerous questions, many of which we consider during the coming chapters and that is why you need to be as sure as you can be of your priorities in respect of your retirement income.

The canvas of questions

There are other significant factors to add into the mix before you can begin to really paint a picture of your personal priorities. For a start, are you married or do you have a partner you need to provide for either now or after your death if you predecease them? Do you have any other financial dependents, parents, elderly relatives or kids that are eternal students? Grandchildren that you would like to help through university or onto the property ladder?

What is the state of your health? Do you have any medical conditions that could reduce your natural lifespan? Not just things like diabetes and high blood pressure, but consider simpler lifestyle factors; are you overweight, do you drink, smoke or go bungee jumping? Again face facts, smokers die on average 5 years before non-smokers so plan your budget according to your lifestyle.

What can your family history tell you about the future? Are you from a family of centenarians or does your clan tend to live fast and die young? There are now several morbid computer programmes on the internet that will let you input all these factors and give you a guesstimate of your longevity, it may be useful to some people as is genetic testing for the same reason, but you could just as easily get hit by a bus as you leave the genetics lab joyous in the news you were going to live to be 100.

These things are contributing factors, not certainties, but you are starting to paint a picture of your life so you can begin to make some informed decisions about your needs and desires for the next phase.

What are your views on work? You may want to work part time and that will produce an income, but realistically how much are you going to earn? How many years are you going to be fit, willing and able to continue? You might want to get away from your current occupation completely, or undertake some form of consultancy, or simply take a stress-free job that allows you to meet people on a daily basis. You may want to undertake some form of voluntary work which by definition has no financial benefit to you, you may want to do a combination and gently slide into retirement over a number of years.

All of these things provide the mental infrastructure to help determine your priorities; do you need to take your Pensions now? Or could you defer, and how much better off would you be as a result? At what age can you take your State Pension, again what are the benefits of deferring it? What will be the net impact on your income as a result of the increased/decreased amount of income tax you will be paying as a result of your priorities?

Timescale

When you really start to think about your priorities, your income requirements and how they are going to be met inevitably you need to consider a realistic timescale, and if the average 60 year old can expect to live for another 20+ years, can we really budget for that, bearing in mind all the likely changes that are going to occur over that time? I think it would be an ambitious man who said he could do so with any accuracy, even if all the external economic assumptions you make regarding interest rates, inflation and investment returns turn out to be true (and you will be an economic genius if they do!)

There are an unimaginable number of personal changes that could blow you off your carefully plotted financial course but you need to be as accurate as you can be and, like all good financial plans, it will be subject to regular review. If your course has been plotted with all the factors thoughtfully calculated you should only need to trim your sails every so often, if you set off on your retirement voyage with only minimal planning you are continually going to be making radical adjustments and these will be a major waste of time, energy, and almost certainly money.

Many people delay doing the things they've dreamed of when they retire because they are afraid of running out of money in later years. In doing so you then run the risk of missing the opportunity to enjoy your money to the full while you are in good health or your partner passes away before you have lived your retirement dream. Keep this in mind in relation to your financial priorities when considering timescales as you may want to plan for your assets to deliver additional income in the early years. I could give you a boatload of examples of clients in their 80s and 90s with thousands in the bank that they will never spend, but they postponed spending it early in retirement, just in case. Now is the time for you to start thinking about spending and living rather than saving and dying.

Income; priorities and choices

Ask yourself, what is my number one financial priority? The most common answer I receive to that question is, "the maximum income possible" – a perfectly feasible priority, to which I may respond, "in that case we need to arrange A, B and C which will mean we have to invest in high-risk stock markets and all the associated uncertainty that comes with that." At which point I hear the screeching of mental brakes often followed by the statement "but I don't want to take any risk" – another perfectly feasible priority but one that is to some degree in direct conflict with priority number one – maximum income. You see it's not that simple is it?

First you need to consider what you actually need for income to meet the fixed costs on your Me plc Profit and Loss Account along with the liabilities on your Me plc Balance Sheet. Then we can look towards what level of income you would *like* and define priorities on that basis. Three holidays may be a priority for one partner, Sky Sports a priority for the other, some tough choices need to be made, but only after the means to meet the necessities have been dealt with.

So back to priorities; what are the most popular ones I encounter after maximum income and capital security? Next on the agenda is certainly freedom of choice and flexibility, issues of control. These are increasingly important for people and are a symptom of the wider choices and flexibility we have in so many aspects of our lives that even 20 years ago would have been unthinkable. We no longer want to simply accept what we are given after decades of being told what to do by employers or the stresses of running a business. We want the simple but eminently desirable goal of being able to choose how we spend our income and how we spend our lives.

The U-shaped income curve

To be clear in your priorities you should establish financial objectives for the short, medium and longer-term which should neatly merge to present a coherent strategy for the long haul.

Income in retirement tends to follow a U-shaped pattern; high during the early years, dropping and levelling off during the middle period of retirement and rising again in later years.

The early years tend to be expensive as you travel and indulge all those hobbies you have been meaning to get around to. The length of this period depends upon a number of factors, the most important, apart from money, being your state of health, but as a general rule consider this period as the first 10 years of your retirement.

The middle period of your retirement – the bottom of our income 'U' if you will - is the time when you will have slowed down, no longer working, reducing your levels of physical activity, enjoying your well-earned rest and spending longer periods at home. If you retired at 60 this could well be the period from 70-80 but there is no fixed term, evidenced by the fact that the over 70s now account for the fastest-growing percentage of travel insurance claims on extreme sports holidays. However, for those that have packed away the hang glider for the last time, it is a period when many people find that for the first time in their lives they actually have more money than they need.

The third period of retirement sees our financial needs begin to rise again, up the right hand curve of our 'U' as we need more assistance, home helps, medical aids, carers, and possibly fulltime nursing or residential care. As our priorities change so do our financial requirements and this is why it is important to retain a flexibility of income and choices as to how and where you invest your assets.

You will not be spending the same at 85 as you were at 65 and at 95 your budget may well be different again, so why elect for a fixed income for life at age 65? In my view you should focus your resources to meet your very personal priorities, there is no right answer as everyone is different, but if you elect to maximize your income when you and your partner are fit and well, say age 60-75 and then run the risk of a reduced income at 85, how critical would that be to your overall retirement plans?

Scoring goals

It is reported that humans are happiest when they are setting and pursuing goals, however little or large, mundane or magnificent they might be. Retirement brings a once in a lifetime opportunity to re-evaluate your life and decide what you want to do with your future and goal setting can play an important part in this. We have looked at your financial priorities, and many of those could be considered goals, it is equally important to consider your very personal non-financial goals too. For them to have a greater chance of being achieved it is sensible to apply the SMART principles in that all your goals must be Specific, Measurable, Achievable, Results orientated and Time based.

Your goals can be as simple or as complex as you want them to be, but they need to be written down, otherwise they are not goals they are only dreams. Perhaps for the first time in your life you have a blank canvas for your time, and learning to paint could be one of your goals, so take full advantage and think BIG!

List them all; from lose 10lbs (by when? how?) tidy the attic, study for a degree (more than 600,000 Open University students are over 60) join a Salsa club, read *War and Peace*, climb the Eiger, knit a jumper or have sex in a hammock. It doesn't matter as long as they mean something to you and fit the SMART criteria. These goals are just as important as your financial objectives and will prove just as beneficial to your long term mental and physical well being as planning your finances.

You should also consider more tangible and longer term objectives such as leaving an inheritance for grandchildren or money to a favourite charity. When making a list of all your goals, financial and non-financial, this exercise could take weeks, but it doesn't matter, make your Goal sheet a living document constantly changing and evolving, but never being allowed to fade and die.

By the side of every goal you write down establish a timescale: short term, that is a goal to be achieved during the next 12 months;

medium, the next 1-5 years and long-term is anything beyond that. Besides each goal, if there is a financial cost then document it and these figures can then be considered in tandem with your other financial priorities.

Finally...

Upon completing this exercise you will now hopefully have your list of financial priorities, know how much you are worth and have a firm indication of not only what you are going to need to live but what you would like in the form of income to not only survive but positively thrive and achieve all the things you would like to do during your retirement. It can be the best of times and the worst of times but a strong financial audit like the one you have just completed will set you off more sure-footedly along the retirement path.

You should now be seeing a long-term financial plan beginning to form and some clarity of purpose should begin to materialize as we look to the next stage of your *Pension Matters* journey. Your plan should be like grandma's nightdress in that it covers everything and is designed to last a lifetime. I am sure you have discovered it is not just your lifespan but your healthspan and wealthspan that play an equally important role in determining your priorities. The choices you make at retirement will affect the rest of your life and that of your significant other if you have one, clarifying your priorities at the start will help you make the right ones.

3 Your birthright; a twisted history

The State Pension

Pensions have been around since Ancient Greece and by the look of the Greek economy they're still paying for them. As a modern European concept it was Bismarck, the original Iron Chancellor of Prussia, who introduced the system as we understand it today, recognition that the State had a moral responsibility towards those that had contributed to their country to ensure they were regarded in their old age.

A twisted history

Our own system was the brainchild of David Lloyd George, a Liberal Chancellor who declared that from the beginning of 1909 'men of good character' with incomes of less than £21 per year would be entitled to a means-tested sum of between one and five shillings per week upon reaching the age of 70. As life expectancy for men at the turn of the 20th century was 48 this was hardly a universal benefit to be enjoyed by all, nor was it a strain on the Exchequer. It did, for the first time, however, introduce the idea of a universal retirement age and replaced the previous system of work until you could physically work no more and then quietly starve to death.

Against a background of social reform and the industrial power of the Labour party, the State Pension began to take on a life of its own, increasing in monetary terms and the age of entitlement reducing to 65, a figure that to this day we still refer to as 'retirement age' even though such an idea is rapidly being, well, retired, for a multitude of reasons, not least the ever-rising number of candles needed on the birthday cake for access to the Basic State Pension.

The biggest boost to the State Pension was the birth of the modern Welfare State after World War II and the National Insurance Act of

1946. This made the State Pension an integral part of the contract between working people and the State. Born out of the premise that there would be a minimum level of financial support for those who were retired, this was to be the level below which no civilized country like Great Britain would allow its retired citizens to fall.

As all workers were now contributing to Pensions in the form of National Insurance there was, and still is, a perfectly reasonable expectation that if you had contributed all of your working life to a Pension scheme you would hopefully avoid dying of hypothermia in your old age.

So what are you actually entitled to? How? When? And why do you get it? What choices do you have in respect of your State Pension? You will have to forgive me for the brief history lesson above and unfortunately there is another one coming along in a minute, but to understand where you are today we need to look at how you, individually, and we collectively as a State, arrived at the present state of affairs.

Another history lesson – back to the future II

This short lesson in history will hopefully help you understand how your own individual Pension amount is calculated. Although there is regular debate regarding the 'Basic State Pension' which in the current tax year (2010/11) is £97 per week, very few people actually receive that set amount and by looking at the history of the system in parallel with a history of your own working life you will hopefully have a clearer understanding of how much you are likely to receive and the reasons for that.

The noble idea that all those paying into the National Insurance fund were providing, amongst other things, Pensions for the elderly, was quietly abandoned in the 1950s. In a similar way that the road tax you pay on your car was designed with the very sensible idea that it would contribute to the upkeep of the road network, this idea has been quietly discarded by a succession of politicians with all those millions disappearing into that murky pool known as general taxation.

So it has become with National Insurance and the provision of welfare benefits. National Insurance is income tax by any other name with its payment rates manipulated to suit the current political agenda, seeking to raise more cash for the Exchequer without slaughtering that most sacred of Political Manifesto cows – no increase in the basic rate of income tax.

The relationship between State Pensions and National Insurance, whilst fractured, is still an essential part of the Pensions system because when and how you paid National Insurance will determine the level of State Pension you, and possibly also your Spouse, will receive from State Pension Age for the rest of your life. As 31% of UK Pensioners have no other income than the State Pension its importance in retirement planning cannot be overestimated.

Women and the State Pension

The State Pension Age is currently 65 for men, (rising to 66 in 2020), for women it is gradually rising from 60 to 65 between now and December 2018, and then jumping to 66 by April 2020 to bring it in line with that of men. If you are unsure of what age you will be entitled to your State Pension there is a super little calculator at www.direct.gov.uk which will tell you your very own personal retirement date.

If you happen to be female you may be doubly disadvantaged if you took time off work to bring up children as you received no NI credit and even if you were working maybe you elected to pay the Married Women's Stamp (a reduced rate of National Insurance that was abolished in 1977) as you didn't need a Pension of your own as you would have one of those big strong men to look after you in retirement.

The Married Women's Stamp penalized the modest NI saving you made each week by denying you the right to accrue State Pension benefits in your own right, permanently undermining your retirement income. If you are married and your NI record is so patchy that you are only entitled to a State Pension of less than £58.50 per week you can claim a Pension based upon your husband's NI contribution record when he retires (you see those big strong men did come in handy eventually). If you are already receiving a Pension of less than £58.50 when your husband receives his Pension the Pensions Service should automatically increase your State Pension to this level.

Similarly if you are divorced and not entitled to a full basic Pension you may be able to use your former Spouse's contributions to increase the basic Pension up to the current maximum of £97.65 per week.

Despite the proposed changes taking place by 2020 and period of relative Pensions calm thereafter, most commentators are of the belief this will be insufficient to diffuse the Pensions time bomb and State Pension Ages are likely to have to rise significantly, to age 70 and beyond. If you are retiring today of course it's not really your problem; other than having to continue contributing to the ever-increasing tax burden of funding state Pensions.

What you need for maximum Basic State Pension

When it was introduced the State Pension system was, by Government standards, straightforward. To qualify for the full amount men had to contribute for 49 years and women for 44 (this is now 30 years for both sexes). Assuming that you made contributions in the traditional way (they were deducted from your pay before you got it whether you liked it or not!), you would accrue a very modest percentage of the Basic State Pension for every year you worked and contributed. You must have contributed for at least 25% or more of your qualifying years to receive the minimum state Pension of £35 per week (2010/11)

If for whatever reason you only worked for 20 years you would accrue a Basic State Pension based upon that proportion, but if you contributed for less than 11 of your qualifying years you will be entitled to nothing at all. For those that are without a full NI contribution record, which is an ever-increasing number as the jobs market becomes more fluid, a series of means-tested benefits are available to bring income up to minimum State Pension level.

For all his many documented faults Gordon Brown introduced changes in 2006 to make qualification for the Basic State Pension easier and simpler. You now only need to have contributed for 30 years to receive a full Basic State Pension and if you are not in a position to contribute you may be amongst many categories of people that can still be credited with NI contributions, thereby helping people like carers and recent mothers achieve a full contribution record even though their personal circumstances preclude them from working.

For more information on the weekly NI credit for people caring for children or those severely disabled, see www.direct.gov.uk/en/Pensionsandretirementplanning.

Buying additional Pension from the State

If your National Insurance record is chequered as a result of bringing up children, unemployment, or going self-employed you always have the opportunity to make single payments to the Department of Work and Pensions to gain NI credit for those lost years.

You can find out more about this also at www.direct.gov.uk/en/Pensionsandretirementplanning and once again it involves a simple calculation for you to decide if this is a good value for your hard-earned cash. Every additional year that you purchase at a cost of £626.60 (2010/11) gives you an additional State Pension of £3.25 per week, so with a Government guarantee and index linking it is going to be approximately 4 years before you show a positive return on your investment. Only you can decide if that represents good value for your money. One great unknown in reaching your conclusion is the effect index linking will have on your future Pension income and of course how long you will be around to collect it.

State Pension and inflation

State Pensions currently increase in line with the Retail Prices Index (RPI) to protect Pensioners income against inflation. In 1975 under the stewardship of Barbara Castle, State Pensions were formally linked to average earnings, which tend to rise at twice the rate of prices, thereby giving Pensioners an increase in income in real terms. Mrs Thatcher abandoned the earnings link in 1980 changing it to RPI, with Pensions increasing each April by the amount the RPI increased the previous September, traditionally the lowest month for price increases. This move proved hugely controversial as Pensioner incomes have continued to fall relative to the population as a whole.

There has been a commitment to restore the link to earnings with the Government announcing in June 2010 that as part of its austerity measures State benefits would rise in line with the CPI (Consumer Price Index) which typically rises at a lower rate than RPI and is calculated slightly differently as it excludes housing costs and, significantly, Council Tax, which is a huge expense for many Pensioners. To protect Pensioners against the adverse affects of this change the Chancellor introduced the 'triple lock' whereby State Pensions will increase by either CPI, average earnings or 2.5% whichever is the greater.

State Second Pension

The 2004 Pensions Act coming into force in April 2006 not only made qualification for the Basic State Pension easier, it also introduced a further change to the second tier of State Pensions provision with the end of SERPS (State Earnings Related Pension Scheme) and the introduction of the new State Second Pension, sexily abbreviated to S2P. What does all that mean?

After the introduction of the Basic State Pension it soon became apparent that it was providing only for the most basic existence and that an earnings linked additional layer of Pension income would be beneficial so that recipients could enjoy a standard of living in their retirement that had at least some modest relation to the one they had enjoyed whilst they were working.

As the full State Pension in 1948 was equivalent to 20% of the average weekly wage, even those with full NI contribution records were facing a substantial drop in income as a 65th birthday present. In 1961 the first earnings-related State Pension provision was introduced for employees in the form of the Graduated Pension.

You should note that this and all future related references to second tier State Pensions apply to employees only; if you are self employed, you are as always, on your own apart from the Basic State Pension.

If you were in a Company Pension scheme that was contracted out of the earnings-related Pension, which Company Schemes could choose to do from the start back in 1961, the next section will not apply as your Company Scheme will have taken responsibility for this portion of your retirement income.

For all other employees earning £9-£15 per week, the amount on which National insurance was paid, the Graduated Pension entitled you to a very modest additional tier of State Pension. This system remained in place until the introduction of SERPS (State Earnings Related Pension Scheme) in April 1978.

More generous than its predecessor, SERPS aimed to provide up to 25% (later reduced to 20%) of an employees best 20 years earnings, 50% of which is payable on death to a surviving Spouse. 'Earnings related' was defined as that part of your income upon which you paid full rate NI contributions, the so-called 'middle band earnings', between £97 - £844 per week, (2010/11) giving retirees a maximum second tier State Pension of approximately £160 per week. Of course if your earnings were less than the NI primary threshold these benefits were simply of no benefit, but for those fortunate employees who paid for this new-found wealth via higher rates of National Insurance, an improved standard of living awaits you at State Pension Age.

For those that have accrued S2P benefits, i.e. that were contracted out after April 2006, the system becomes more complicated, if such a thing were possible! In an attempt to introduce a greater element of fairness the new system would not be so earnings-related and the second tier Pension would be applied at a flat rate for all those earning up to £13,900 per annum, with those that were not working but being credited with NI contributions such as those caring for the disabled would also be deemed to be earning £13,900 for the purpose of calculating S2P entitlement.

Hopefully you are now beginning to see how your own Pensions history is intertwined with that of the State and you can understand not only why no two people are necessarily in receipt of the same level of State Pension but why it can be so very difficult to calculate what exactly you are entitled to when State Pension Age arrives.

Calculating your own State Pension

If you don't want to wear out the buttons on your calculator you can avoid this next section by using the State Pension Profiler at www.direct.gov.uk for an online forecast of your Pension benefits or by completing a BR19 form, which can be obtained online or from the Department of Work and Pensions. By doing your own calculations not only will you begin to understand why you are in receipt of the amount that you are, but also it is a valuable cross check against the DWP calculations, who have been known to make the occasional mistake.

BAD NEWS... IT SEEMS TO
BE THE WRONG FORMULA...
THE GOOD NEWS IS THAT YOU'RE
NOW A FROG OF SOLID GOLD
BIG BOOK
OF FINANCIAL
ALGORITHMS

If you want to work out the value of your personal State Pension fund, that is easy, it is zero, the same as it was last year and the year before that because what you pay out of your wages on a Friday as National Insurance is paid out across the Post Office counter as Pension on a Monday. You are never actually accumulating a Pension fund in your own right and your Pension income will be dependent upon the compliance and goodwill of the next generation of workers, the same as current Pensioners are dependent upon your goodwill for their enduring income.

You can begin to calculate what you are likely to receive as State Pension by doing what used to be called, in the days when people smoked, the back of a fag packet calculation. For every full year you made NI contributions until 2006 you will have accrued approximately 2.5% of the Basic State Pension. For every year thereafter approximately 3.3% per year up to a maximum of 100% which can be accrued over 30 years, in return for contributing to the Treasury's coffers to fund those who went before you. When it comes to working out the earnings-related part, things become a little more complex. For the Graduated Pension (employment between April 1961 and April 1978) you will have accrued only a few pence for every year you contributed, so probably not worth worrying about here.

For employment and SERPS contributions between April 1978 and April 2006 things start to get more interesting, first of all you need to work out your best 20 years earnings (usually the most recent 20 years), take an average and then take 20% of those earnings on which you paid National insurance. Multiply this figure by the number of years you were gleefully contributing to the NI fund and this will give you a rough and ready guide to your level of SERPS Pension.

Company Schemes and second tier Pensions

If you have been contracted out of the State second Pension by virtue of your membership of an Occupational Pension scheme, and have enjoyed lower rates of NI contributions as a result, your scheme administrators should be writing to you prior to retirement clearly showing the various elements of your Pension, how they have been accrued, how they will increase, benefits for your Spouse and so forth, so I am not going to enter into the complexities of the various contracting out scenarios within Company Pension schemes – that in itself could fill a book.

If you do have any queries in relation to this aspect of your Company Pension your scheme administrators should be in a position to answer them and if you have any dispute as to how these figures were arrived at you always have recourse to your scheme trustees to resolve the matter.

The Pension Credit (formerly the Minimum Income Guarantee)

Having calculated the amount of your State Pension and deciding you are going to have to cancel that Caribbean cruise, you may take heart that all is not lost. Since 2003 a means-tested benefit has been in place to provide all Pensioners with a minimum level of income, even if they have built up modest amounts of savings and Pensions during their working lives.

The Pension credit, available to those over 60, considers all of your sources of income and the amount of savings you have and, despite the complexity of the application forms, more than 3.5 million Pensioners now benefit to varying degrees from a higher income as a result of the Pension credit.

If your total income is less than the Pension credit level and your savings are less than £6,000 you will be entitled to a benefit designed to bring your minimum income up to £130 per week (2010/11) if you are single or £198.45 for a couple. The Credit is administered through The Pensions Service and you can call the Pension Credit Helpline on 0800 99 1234.

Other benefits

There are other benefits that are available to you once you reach State Pension Age that should not be disregarded - free dental care, if you can find a dentist! Free eye tests, winter fuel allowance and a free TV license for the over 75s.

There are some more obvious tax benefits in that your Personal Allowance (the amount of income you can receive before any liability to income tax) increases at 65 from £6,475 to £9,490, giving you an additional £3,015 (2010/11) of tax-free income. Do remember that your State Pension constitutes earned income and is therefore liable to income tax so needs to be included in any tax computation you may make, not only for your own records to calculate your level of income, but also for our friends at HMRC who don't take kindly to being deprived of their rightful share.

Deferring your State Pension

If you elect to continue working past State Retirement Age or you simply have sufficient funds that you do not need to claim your Basic State Pension you have the opportunity to defer taking it. For every 5 weeks that you defer your Pension it will increase by 1%, so for every year that you wait your Pension will be higher by approximately 10%, not exactly a massive incentive, bearing in mind that the longer you defer the shorter the period that you will receive it.

As your State Pension is liable to income tax you might want to postpone until your tax rate reduces; for example, you may drop from a higher rate tax band to basic rate as a result of stopping work or you may cease from being a tax payer altogether due to increased personal income tax allowances. As deferment could save you 20% tax on that portion of your income it could be something to consider.

Finally...

The simple support mechanism delivered by Lloyd George back in 1909 has taken on a life of its own and a century of tinkering by politicians, some of it well-meaning and some of it not, has left us with a complex Pension situation on an individual level and an ongoing social problem nationally, a situation that no Government has shown any real political courage to resolve. Until one does it is important that you understand where and why you fit into the State Pension system and what options are available to you within it.

I accept that a history of the State Pension is unlikely to make the bestsellers list but hopefully you can understand why I have elected to go into such depth and you should now have a clearer vision of your hard-earned entitlements at State Pension Age. If you have any questions in relation to State Pension Benefits you can contact The Pensions Service which are a part of the Department of Work and Pensions in Newcastle upon Tyne. The main contact number is 0845 60 60 265. Alternatively there is a vast amount of information on their website www.thepensionservice.gov.uk.

4 Tales of sailboats and lifeboats

Company Pensions

An endangered species

Against the ever darkening skies shrouding the Company Pensions landscape there are still some very bright rays of hope shining light and, more importantly, good fortune, on those that have been fortunate enough to benefit from membership of a good Company Pension scheme.

Pension scheme membership is a class issue, or to be politically correct 'closely related to socio-economic status' according to the ONS Wealth and Assets survey. The higher you are up the economic pecking order the more likely you are to be a member of an occupational Pension scheme, so if social status is important to you, tell everyone you know that you are in a Company Pension scheme!

If you are, you certainly have rarity value as you are part of an ever-diminishing elite. In 1967 there were 8.1 million private sector employees in Company-sponsored Pension Schemes; this was down to 3.6 million in 2008 and falling at an alarming rate. The only area where membership is growing is the public sector, up from 4.2 million in 1991 to 5.4 million in 2008 - but we will not pick up that political hot potato.

The achievements of occupational Pensions in the UK should not be underestimated; they have been a tremendous success story for British Companies and their employees. The Government, recognizing the scale of the social service that such schemes provided for Pensioners, have granted numerous tax breaks and concessions in respect of such things as National Insurance and contracting out to encourage the promotion of these schemes which have taken up a substantial amount of the burden that would otherwise have to be borne by the taxpayer.

To give you an indication of the sheer scale of private sector Pension provision in the UK, it has been estimated that the number of UK Pension assets dwarf the combined Pension assets of all other EU member states put together. So take a moment to bask in national pride, at last there is something we can beat the Germans at! Not only the Germans, but France, Spain, Italy, Denmark and all the rest of them put together. If you reflect on that economic fact for a moment you begin to appreciate the sheer scale of the UK Pensions industry and its importance to the UK workforce.

There are currently 15 million people in the UK who are, or at sometime have been, members of Company Pensions which hold combined investment assets of £800 billion. On any scale UK Company Pensions are a colossal economic force and anything that impacts on them not only impacts on the UK economy but also on you if you are a potential recipient of their funds.

Gordon Brown began to undo 50 years of good solid work by British industry in 1997 with his £5bn tax raid on Pension funds, and subsequent legislation over the next 10+ years has left Company Pension Schemes way past the point of no return. There is a widely held belief that Company Pension Schemes as we understand them today will simply not exist in 10 years time.

The statistics themselves make very stark reading and a quick roll call of some of our biggest names gives you a feel of where we are heading. The FTSE 100, that barometer of UK economic wellbeing, reads like a memorial for Company Pensions.

To reduce spiralling costs, schemes initially stopped offering membership to new employees and then began reducing benefits for existing members whilst increasing their level of contributions and raising the retirement age. This Canute-like action was not enough and the trickle of Pension schemes closing has become a flood. Rentokil has the ignominious claim of being the first FTSE 100 Company to close its scheme to current employees which it did in 2007 and whilst you may have thought that you would never see the words Rentokil and trailblazing in the same sentence, they really were carving a path that so many others would soon follow.

So where did it all go wrong?

The repeated actions of Government, both nationally and at European level, have certainly not helped but we are back to Queen Victoria and her telegrams; the biggest problem facing Company Pensions is the annoying fact that we are continuing to live longer than Pension scheme trustees estimated we would. The Actuarial profession, which has the job of analyzing data in relation to all aspects of Pension finance, produces estimates of such things as investment returns and, naturally, longevity. The Government Actuaries Department (GAD) has a particular interest in such things, but such forecasts carry serious flaws, not least that we do not know how long we are going to live until we are dead, so Actuaries are constantly having to use historic data to predict the future.

We all know that we are living longer as a country but how can we predict how much longer? We know that in 1970 the average life expectancy at birth for a British male was 68.7 and 75 for a female. By 2008 this had risen to 77.8 and 81.9 years respectively (Social Trends survey 40). This equates to an increase for men of around one additional year of life every 4 years. So what are the poor old Actuaries meant to do? Look at the last number and add 1 or 4 or 10 years of life?

It is impossible to predict as the advances in medicine and standards of care continue to improve, who would dare forecast the breakthrough of a drug to treat cancer or heart disease, but when it happens it means the Actuaries' carefully calculated forecasts are in the bin.

There has been a widely held belief that the massive leaps in human longevity over the last 50 years will begin to wane as the effects of major medical breakthroughs such as antibiotics begin to reduce and lifestyle factors such as obesity and too much booze begin to take their toll but there is little evidence to support this. A recent study predicted that babies being born in 2010 could reasonably expect to live to be 150 years old; there have even been suggestions that longevity could increase indefinitely so that not-too-distant future generations could be on the planet for 400 years or more.

When you consider that longevity in the UK has almost doubled in little more than a century, what's to stop it doubling again over the next 100 years if the major diseases are conquered by science? Suddenly a 180-year-old Pensioner doesn't seem so outrageous. Any bets for the date that the first person reaches 200? This may be good news for the makers of daytime TV but for the providers of Pensions this is the stuff of nightmares. How do they calculate for an unknown, unquantifiable financial liability? This is the question facing all those employers' final salary Pension schemes.

Regulation, red tape and deficits

Recent regulation has included making Company Pension Schemes more accountable and transparent; having them run by qualified professionals with all schemes contributing a levy to provide a safety net should some of their number fail. Who could argue against such prudent action? Nevertheless, all these measures add costs to running a Pension scheme, costs which must ultimately be borne by the employer. Throw into the mix volatile stock markets with falling investment returns (not to mention longevity again) and the benefits of offering a Pension scheme to employees start to look increasingly unattractive.

Employers have a contractual obligation to fund your Company scheme and whilst you might have been contributing 5% of your salary every month chances are it was costing your employer 3 times that amount, plus they have to pitch another few million into the black hole every so often to try and plug the ever-returning scheme deficit. All this while trying to run a business and ideally remain solvent. Suddenly the whole idea of offering your employees a final salary based Pension scheme looks more than unattractive – it looks like economic madness.

There is much in the press about the collective Pension deficit, and estimates of the liabilities our major Companies face varies from £100bn to £200bn. Some very big numbers, but what does it all mean for you as a member of a scheme with a deficit? Company Schemes are obliged to regularly calculate all the assets and liabilities within their scheme. They value all of their investment holdings, consider all contributions that may be forthcoming, make assumptions about future investment returns, inflation and how long all their members are going to live, then consider how much they are actually committed to paying in Pensions and for how long.

This complex calculation will ultimately tell them in very simple terms if they have sufficient assets to meet all of their future liabilities, or not. If the answer is not then they are said to have a deficit and under current regulations the trustees have to put forward a proposal to the Pensions Regulator as to how they propose to eliminate this deficit and within what timescale, usually 5 years.

There are numerous examples of the Pension scheme deficit being larger than the entire market value of the Company – British Airways being the oft-quoted example that if you sold every plane, building and asset that BA own, right down to the last bottle of duty free and put the proceeds in the Pension scheme there still would not be enough money for the Pension scheme to meet its obligations.

It is examples such as BA (and they are far from alone in their plight) that make you appreciate the sheer size of the problem. As all Pension liabilities have to be openly declared on the Company balance sheet, Pension scheme deficits are becoming so critical that they are having a disproportionate influence on longer-term corporate planning as every decision has to be made against the backdrop of the ever-hungry Pension scheme. One estimate suggests Pension fund liabilities now account for almost 35% of the FTSE100 Companies' total stock market value.

We are now seeing instances of Company buyouts falling at the last hurdle because the potential new owners, quite understandably, did not want to take on the open-ended liability of a Company Pension scheme, WH Smiths and Sainsburys to name but two recent cases.

When was the last time you saw the following four words in the same sentence: Pension. Scheme. Good. News? No, I can't remember either. Not a week goes by without an announcement from a major UK Company of the latest rescue package for their Pension scheme. As I write this Marks and Spencer has announced plans to pump a total of £800m into their Pension scheme in an attempt to fill the growing funding gap. The scheme had a £1.3bn Pension deficit and aims to be back in balance in 8 years. Shareholders will no doubt be relieved that their forgone dividend has gone to a good home.

Now even if you are Richard Branson these are the kind of figures that will make your eyes water and they throw a seriously large spanner into your corporate planning machine.

Consider the poor Company Directors

As an employee or Pensioner, deferred or otherwise, you are naturally well pleased at being a member of a Final Salary Scheme with all the security that will bring you in your retirement, but just for a moment consider your Board of Directors and their position. I am not saying feel sorry for them, I'm just saying consider.

The Company Pension Scheme used to be like the old maiden aunt that sat on the Board of Directors, as long as she was adequately funded and knew she was being looked after along with the employees she was happy to sit quietly and pretty much agree to what her other Directors wanted. Recently however she has become far more awkward and quarrelsome, demanding escalating financial support, asking increasingly difficult questions of the Board of Directors and exerting an influence far out of proportion to her contribution to the long-term corporate strategy of the Company. This is creating resentment and causing difficulties to such an extent that the rest of the Board would actually like to see the back of her and some have even quietly discussed the possibility of killing her off completely!

As your Directors sit forlornly staring at the latest set of Pension accounts lying before them on the polished boardroom table, considering writing yet another cheque for £x million pounds, it does not take an accounting genius to ask the profound question, "why on earth do we keep on doing this?"

As the sharpest financial minds cannot find a sound commercial answer to our simple question, and providing a valuable benefit for our loyal and hard working employees is not considered a sound commercial answer, the closure of Final Salary Schemes is having a domino effect. The Financial Services Authority became the latest employer to take this step telling its 500 staff that it will no longer pay into their Final Salary Scheme, and if the FSA don't know what the future holds financially who does? Other big names that have already taken this step include Fujitsu, IBM, Morrisons, Vodafone, Taylor Wimpey, Barclays and finally insurance giant Aviva, describing its £3bn deficit as 'simply unsustainable'.

If you need any more reasons to understand why Final Salary Schemes are going the way of the Brontosaurus consider the following facts, extracted from The Pension Protection Fund's Purple Book published in January 2010:

- 5,900 Pension schemes (85%) are in deficit;, to the tune of approx £200bn
- Every time life expectancy increases by 2 years, a scheme's liabilities increase by 5%

- 73% of all Final Salary Schemes are now closed completely

If all of that doesn't even make you shiver, absorb this next killer statistic from the same source:

- For every 100 scheme members 36 are Pensioners, 43 are deferred members (those that have left but will be entitled to a Pension in the future) only 23 out of every 100 Pension scheme members are actively employed and paying into the scheme.

You don't need to be a mathematical genius to work out the improbability of such a system being around for too long.

Once you hear the loud clang of the door shutting on the accumulation of Pension benefits for active members, the next sound you will hear is the clock gently ticking away the time towards the inevitable conclusion; the scheme being bought by an insurance Company or one of the new so-called 'Pension consolidators.'

These are Companies that take over all the assets and liabilities of your Pension scheme and become responsible for payments of your Pensions in the future. This removes the Pensions headaches permanently for the Company Directors, takes the liability off the balance sheet and means your Pension is in the hands of a business that has taken it on, not to ensure that you receive what you are morally and legally entitled to, but because it believes it can squeeze a profit out of it. Not a pleasant thought but perhaps you are still in safer hands than with your employer who may go bust at anytime, leaving the scheme for the Pension Protection Fund to manage.

Pension Protection - A story of sailboats and lifeboats

Robert Maxwell took a belly flop off his yacht into the sea around Tenerife in November 1991 and the ripples from his fall are still being felt today, and not because he was an overweight tub of lard. When it came to light that he had 'borrowed' £460 million from the Mirror Group Pension fund to support his ailing business empire the effect on his employees' retirement plans was devastating. Many had worked all their lives for the Mirror Group, and apart from the massive financial loss, the distress this caused to thousands of people is incalculable. The irony is that Maxwell could have borrowed from the Pension fund quite legitimately providing he had the permission of the trustees; something a man of his reputation should have not had any difficulty in obtaining. It was and still is, a frequent occurrence, for sponsoring employers to use their Pension funds as a source of capital to fund their business plans. This can make good economic sense for all parties including the Pension scheme members who will hopefully see a healthy return on their loan to the Company concerned. The trouble was that all too often the Pension Scheme trustees were also senior employees of the Company with no real independence, expertise or authority to decline any requests for loans to the employer. Whilst many of these loans were genuine commercial arrangements, Maxwell was by no means alone in using his Company's Pension fund as his personal piggy bank to take a hammer to as and when he chose.

The 1995 Pensions Act took some steps towards protecting members of Company Schemes against fraud and dishonesty, establishing the Occupational Pensions Regulatory Authority (OPRA) in 1997 to act as guardian and regulator. Although OPRA had a range of powers, they were insufficient to protect members' interests completely, not least as there was no way to separate Pension fund assets in the case of employer insolvency or to protect members if the Pension Scheme was wound up with a shortfall. What was not helpful during the post-Maxwell period was the Government repeatedly issuing reassurances that Final Salary Schemes were 'guaranteed' - no mention of the danger of schemes winding up with shortfalls.

Launch the lifeboats!

This level of protection wouldn't come until much later but the major step forward in defending scheme members against the effects of insolvency came with the arrival of the Pension Protection Fund and its predecessor the Financial Assistance Scheme (FAS) launched by the Government in May 2004 with a funding of £400m.

The FAS was designed to help members of underfunded schemes that had been wound up between January 1997 and April 2005, but as with all lifeboats there was no travelling in luxury. Pensions paid by FAS have no Spouse's or dependents' benefits and are not protected against inflation. Also the maximum that is paid out is far from generous.

Maximum payout for those with less than 7 years to retirement is 80% of their benefits and this percentage reduces the further you are away from retirement down to 50% if you are more than 12 years away, so at least you have long enough to get over the shock of a 50% loss to your Pension. The FAS was improved in May 2006 but was still quite rightly accused of being inadequate so the Government launched a slightly more luxurious craft in the form of The Pension Protection Fund (PPF).

Schemes can apply to the PPF to rescue them if they are all at sea financially and the Company providing the Pension, your employer, has become insolvent. The scheme enters an assessment period, which lasts a minimum of 12 months during which time investigations are made and the possibility of the scheme being able to stand on its own two feet is considered. In the vast majority of cases this will prove unlikely and the scheme will then be placed under the long-term supervision of the PPF.

There is one very important point to note regarding the beginning of the assessment period. No matter when the scheme applies to the PPF for help, the assessment period is deemed to have begun the day the Company went bust. Why does this matter? Simply because once a scheme has entered a PPF assessment period transfers out of the scheme are no longer permitted.

Keep in mind that the PPF is NOT underwritten by the Government, its continuation depends upon the collection of a levy from solvent Pension Schemes. As these continue to diminish in number the financial responsibility of those remaining will spiral, placing them under yet more financial pressure, an ever-decreasing vicious circle that at some point in the future has to implode.

The very first schemes to apply to the PPF for assessment in 2005 were Pension schemes run by Heath Lambert who were insurance brokers and would you believe it, Pension advisers. Now these guys should really know their way around the red tape of Pensions regulation better than most, yet administrative and legal problems delayed the assessment process and it has taken 5 years for the schemes to be finally accepted into the PPF and members' Pensions secured. Yes, I did say 5 years.

Real life...

Alan Mitchell and I sat in his office on Teesside discussing the merits of transferring out of the Artenius Pension scheme. Artenius was previously part of ICI, a Company with a proud history of providing excellent Pension provision for its employees. But things had changed, Artenius, owned by Spanish giant Grupo Seda, was facing increasingly strong competition from the Far East, there had already been redundancies, and the inevitable Pension deficit was causing concern.

Alan had been made redundant from Artenius some months previously, was just about to turn 50 and had decided early retirement was an attractive option. We had a previous discussion and I had encouraged him to think long and hard before taking such a step, pointing out that he was forgoing a guaranteed index-linked Pension at 62 in exchange for a much smaller and risk-laden Pension today.

Alan was adamant, "Not bothered, don't trust them. I have plans for the future and none of those plans feature the Artenius Pension Scheme," he stated, pointing out the window towards the giant Artenius plant across the field no more than a mile or so away. So, agreeing to undertake the transfer, I went through all the downsides and completed the standard backside-covering exercise of getting him to sign that he understood all the risks and on his own head be it. We shook hands and parted at 11.30am with me once more reminding him that he would have up to 3 months to change his mind as that's how long Pension schemes can take to write a transfer cheque.

I need not have worried as events down the road had already changed his mind for him. As we had sat working through the pile of forms required to move Alan's money into the shark-infested waters of the stock market, him calculating his tax-free cash, me calculating my fee, we couldn't have been happier. Unfortunately less than a mile away the Director of Artenius was up on his metaphorical soap box announcing that the Company was to be placed into administration.

Hearing this on the midday news as I drove back to the office I knew what this meant for Alan's proposed transfer.

Of course transfers ceased immediately and the Artenius Pension is in a period of PPF assessment. Alan remains stuck in the Artenius Pension Scheme until his normal retirement age of 62. No early retirement, no tax-free cash, no choice.

Despite Alan's protestations to the scheme, his solicitor, his MP and anyone else in the pub who would listen, Alan and 200,000 members of the 201 schemes in PPF assessment are stuck until their scheme retirement age. Despite Alan's understandable grievance that all his retirement plans have been hijacked by the PPF, they are providing an extremely valuable support service to members of failing schemes, even if it does mean Alan has to wait until he is 62 to appreciate it.

The average scheme entering the PPF has a funding level of 70%, so the best those scheme members could have hoped for would be a 30% loss in Pension, coupled with a lot of uncertainty about the future, up to retirement and beyond. The PPF helps restore some of that certainty that Company Pension Schemes were supposed to provide in the first place. If you should become an unwilling member of the PPF you are assured of receiving a substantial proportion of your Pension benefits at retirement age, up to 90% (but it could be less!) to a maximum of £29,748 (2010/11) per year, and there is a modest amount of index linking up to 2.5% for benefits built up after April 1997.

In 2008/09 the PPF paid out a massive £37.6 billion in benefits with an average payment of £3,765, which may not seem a fortune but for many it will be the difference between survival and a reasonable standard of living. As I said, it is no luxury liner on which you would choose to spend your retirement, but it is a very valuable lifeboat and could make the difference between swimming and drowning.

What exactly are Company Pensions?

We are going to consider the main types of scheme, how they work, what they can do for you and what you can do with them. Once again some simple calculations will provide you with a guideline figure as to what you can expect at retirement, or if you are already at retirement provide a valuable cross check of what you can expect to be in receipt of for the rest of your natural.

Final Salary Schemes

The actual value of your Pension in retirement is directly related to your salary at the date of leaving the scheme (or reaching normal retirement age if you remain in the scheme). Your salary when you left or retired is coupled with the length of your service with the Company to arrive at your Pension income. Each and every day of Pensionable service you accrue additional rights under the scheme which increases the value of your Pension income.

Real life…

Mike left his former employer and his salary was £20,000, the accrual rate under the scheme was 1/60th, which means for every year of service Mike would build up a Pension of 1/60th of his final salary. If he completed 10 years' service he would have accrued Pension benefits of £3,333.33 (£20,000 divided by 60 multiplied by 10 years).

These benefits will never normally be reduced and will increase each year between the date of Mike leaving his former employer and retiring by a modest amount each year to allow for inflation (up to a maximum of 5%). Mike's Pension benefits will not fluctuate in value and not be subject to the vagaries of the investment markets.

'Money Purchase' Schemes

Although provided by your caring employer who makes a generous contribution every month in to your Pension fund, the actual value of your Pension in retirement is dependent upon investment returns between now and your retirement date. Unlike final salary schemes your income in retirement will not be related to your salary at retirement or the date of you leaving the scheme.

Your former employer's scheme trustees will have allocated contributions on your behalf and take responsibility for the investment and management of your Pension fund. They must exercise due care, but there is ultimately no guarantee as to the level of income you will receive when you retire, although 'lifestyling' (see below) may have been applied or you may be able to influence returns by making fund choices yourself if your scheme allows it.

Money Purchase Schemes will generally fall into two camps; the larger ones will appoint an investment manager such as one of the large merchant banks or fund managers who will be given a mandate outlining their responsibilities and what is expected of them in terms of investment returns. More modest size schemes tend to delegate responsibility to an insurance Company or fund house such as Fidelity, who will offer a range of funds or portfolios for investors (that's you!) to choose from.

Virtually all will offer a default fund or investment strategy so for those members of the scheme that have neither the time nor inclination to spend their Sunday afternoons analyzing investment funds, they will automatically be placed in the default fund, otherwise known as the fund choice for those that don't actively make a choice!

Lifestyling

This is a fine example of creative thinking on behalf of insurance Companies and does, of course, have absolutely nothing to do with your lifestyle, but despite the misnomer it is a very valuable function within many Money Purchase Pension Schemes, as well as Personal and Stakeholder plans.

Lifestyling is based upon the premise that your appetite for risk will decrease with age and that the nearer you get to your chosen retirement date the less likely it is you will want to take a risk with your accumulated funds. Risk is a vital part of any investment strategy, but as you approach the hallowed ground of retirement you will probably not want to be invested in the Japanese stock market. There are numerous variations of lifestyling and I will keep it simple here, but the chart below demonstrates how your funds can be gradually switched into lower risk investments as you near your own magical retirement date.

10 Year Lifestyle Investment Programme

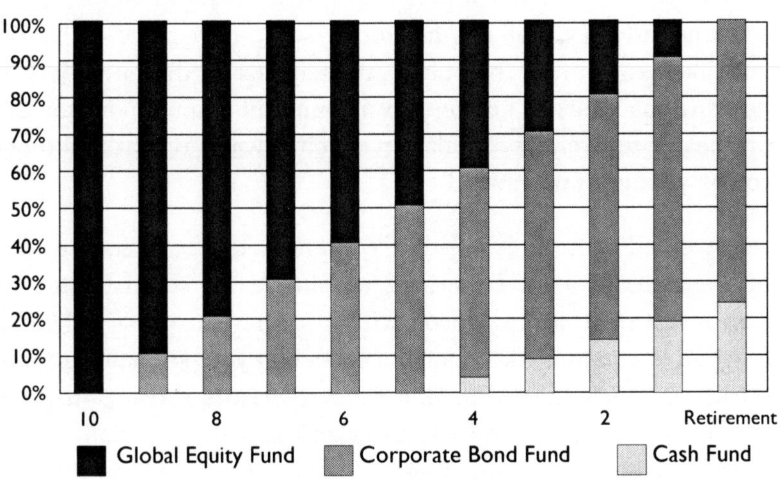

You may well have a choice of funds or portfolios to choose from and some brief explanations of these will have been provided by your scheme but at the final count investment returns will be the main determinant of the size of your fund when you reach that chosen birthday.

Traditionally, default funds for Money Purchase Schemes tended to be Global Equity funds with a mix of Bonds blended in to provide some diversity. For instance if you were 30 years old your portfolio might be 90% Global Equities and 10% Bonds, by the time you reach retirement those percentages would have gradually been reversed to consolidate any gains you have made and protect your Pension fund against any adverse stock market movements as you near retirement.

The next generation of Money Purchase schemes

Money Purchase Schemes are becoming increasingly sophisticated offering complex-sounding facilities such as capital guaranteed decumulation specific target dated funds. It is not widely publicized but every year the Pensions industry holds an awards ceremony and one of the most coveted prizes is the Contrary to Recognized Actual Principles award which is awarded to the member of the Pensions industry that has fashioned some new piece of jargon most likely to confuse the public and help ensure that members of the Pensions industry are kept in meaningful employment for the foreseeable future. 'Decumulation specific' was a recent and most worthy winner of this award.

Target dated options is another contender that is creeping into the Pensions lexicon. Described as 'simple yet sophisticated' it is an investment strategy used within Money Purchase Schemes designed to aim for retirement in a particular year, so that everyone retiring in 2020 will be in one fund, everyone retiring in 2021 another slightly more volatile fund and so on. Essentially these are more sophisticated methods of lifestyling and disregarding the inevitable jargon that accompanies these innovations they are to be welcomed as they provide members with more choice and a more individual approach to their own retirement needs.

Guaranteed Minimum Pension (GMP)

If your scheme has been contracted out, as is usually the case, your Pension will be composed of several elements which may increase at different rates before and after retirement and it is important that you comprehend how these figures are arrived at.

GMP replaces the second tier of the State Pension so instead of being entitled to SERPS, your GMP, which is largely composed of NI rebates, will compensate you for not being a recipient of the many varieties of second tier State Pension provision. There is a useful clue in the name as to what you can expect from it and this guarantee is a contractual obligation made by the trustees in return for being allowed to opt out of the State scheme and avoid the associated National Insurance cost.

Once in payment your GMP will rise in line with inflation up to a maximum of 5% each year, the majority of which is funded by the DWP in combination with your employer. If you were contracted out after April 1997, things start to get a little more murky as GMP no longer accrues after that date so your contracted out benefits are referred to as Section 9(2)b Rights or Protected Rights, I won't get into all that here but effectively you will receive a Pension that will be index-linked up to a maximum of 2.5% for all of your contracted out service after April 1997.

Anything that isn't related to contracting out is usually referred to as 'excess', what you might call your Pension proper and usually constitutes the largest portion. This also benefits from certain guarantees, but the extent of them will be determined by your scheme rules rather than regulations which is the case with GMP so there can be huge variance between schemes but they will be documented in your scheme booklet, or in more detail in the Scheme Trust Deed and Rules if you fancy some seriously heavy reading.

‘Excess’ Pension Benefits

As a general rule your Pension can be index linked up to a maximum of 5% per annum, but this may reduce for benefits accrued after April 2002, down to 2.5%. There may also be ‘discretionary increases’ awarded by the trustees to Pensioners over their statutory requirements. If there are sufficient funds in the scheme or it is in surplus the trustees may make a decision to award an increase to your income in retirement which over many years can be very valuable. Although as I am sure you can appreciate, due to the parlous state of Company Pensions discretionary increases have become something of an endangered species in recent years.

Should you predecease your Spouse or civil partner they will usually be entitled to a Pension for life of 50% of whatever you were receiving at the time of your death. This can be as much as 66% or even 100%, but half is the norm. Once again this is index linked for the duration of your Spouse’s or civil partner’s life, but remember unless you are legally bound together your partner will get nothing. The fact that you may have lived together for many years, have children together or have sworn your undying love for each other counts for nothing in the eyes of Pension scheme trustees unless you have that legal document binding you together as a couple in the eyes of the law.

Deferred Pensioners

If you have built up Company Pension benefits and have left prior to taking your Pension, you are what is known as a ‘deferred member’. If you should die in that deferred state, and have no Spouse then in the largest majority of cases your Pension fund will die with you, no one will benefit from your years of hard graft. So if you are single or divorced and on Monday you have a Company Pension with a value of £200,000, Monday night you get hit by the number 9 bus, Tuesday your Pension is worth zero and your £200,000 goes back into the pot for the benefit of other members in the scheme, not into your estate. Thank you very much.

With ever-increasing divorce rates and more people choosing to live together than take the leap into the marital unknown this is proving a very real problem. Pension scheme trustees who have a legal as well as moral obligation to act in the best interests of all their members face increasingly difficult decisions in respect of unmarried members Pensions who die in deferment.

Real Life...

Derek was divorced after 22 years of marriage and decided it was time for a fresh start in every area of his life, so after 20 years service with a High Street Bank he decided to give up his secure salary (and Pension) and join the ranks of the self employed as a finance broker for business. With all his contacts the business ticked along quite nicely and accepting the fact that he would never be a millionaire he was glad to be away from the stress of working for a large organization.

Derek set up a personal Pension and started paying in £300 per month and at the same time asked me to look into his old Bank Pension. We established that his Pension fund would be worth £322,493 if he chose to transfer it away, but of course if he did so he would lose all the benefits of a quality Final Salary Scheme. We agreed to keep the matter under review and then fate intervened in the form of throat cancer. Derek began to make plans but it was too late, bitter in the knowledge that his children, who were grown up and therefore not financially dependent, would not benefit from £322,493 of Pension fund that was going to pass away with him.

5 Should I stay or should I go?

Transferring your Company Pension

Frozen or just a little chilly?

One of the great misnomers of Company Pensions is the repeated references to 'frozen' Pensions as in, "I've got a Pension with Iceland and of course it's frozen". The implication being that the Pension in question is somehow suspended in time and space, unchanging until it is magically thawed out as your retirement date approaches and it is paid to you. For anyone leaving their Company Pension scheme after 1st January 1986 this has simply not been the case. Your Pension will have been calculated at the date of leaving the scheme and then be revalued annually to allow for inflation each and every year until retirement age. The amount of revaluation will depend upon a number of factors; if your scheme was contracted out then the GMP element of your preserved Pension will be revalued at a fixed rate every year regardless of inflation and that fixed rate will be determined by your leaving date.

The remainder of your Pension (the excess) will be revalued at a level determined by the scheme rules up to a maximum of 5% per year, although some schemes are considerably less generous and of course there is the risk that inflation runs higher than 5% for a prolonged period, but this has not been an issue in recent years.

Be certain what you have

Your annual benefit statement will provide you with a projection of what your Pension at retirement is estimated to be and people can get quite enthusiastic when they see what can be quite large numbers, particularly if you are a long way from the scheme retirement date. Try to focus on the 'Pension at date of leaving' figure as this will provide you with a healthy reality call. Why?

Because this is the basis for your Pension income and the future projection is making certain assumptions about the rate of inflation between now and your retirement. These may or may not turn out to be true, but my point is that your Pension is not going to be worth any more in real spending power terms than on the day you left. Yes it will never go down and yes it will keep pace with inflation (up to 5%) but it is never going to increase in true value. Your £5,000 Pension at the date of leaving may be estimated to be £15,000 when you are 60 but between now and then the cost of living may well have trebled as well!

The advantage of index linking as a benefit is not to be underestimated, but it does need to be placed in the context of the real inflationary world. Your Pension benefits will certainly not be frozen, perhaps a little chilly as the cold wind of inflation whips around your Pension's more exposed regions but certainly not frozen as we used to understand it.

Should I stay or should I go?

If you want to see your Pension potentially grow in real terms or you would like to flex your Pension freedom rather than remain in a secure arena of a Final Salary Scheme, what can you do? Transfer your fund into a Personal or Stakeholder Pension plan is one popular option.

Moving out of the safe harbour of Company Pension Schemes into the stormy waters of Personal Pensions requires very, very careful consideration by you and very stringent analysis by your Adviser. This is certainly not a move to be made without some very long conversations with your Adviser and some in depth soul searching about what you really want from your Pension Scheme. Why the serious tone here? Two very good reasons:

1. It is a once-in-a-lifetime decision; once the transfer is complete there is no going back.

   NOT EVER.

2. The decision you have made will impact on your income for the rest of your life and maybe even beyond that.

For the two reasons above Pension transfers are a hugely contentious issue and they have a history. In the late 1980s, actively encouraged by the Government and cheered on by insurance Companies, millions of people were advised to leave their perfectly good Company Pensions and transfer into a shiny new Personal Pension.

The Government actually ran TV ads showing some poor chap struggling to get out of a straightjacket with a comforting voiceover preaching the benefits of leaving your Company Scheme. Insurance Companies who are never shy of a money-making opportunity encouraged members of these schemes to free themselves from their metaphorical Pensions' straightjacket and enjoy the new-found freedoms that only Personal Pensions could give them.

These freedoms included such treats as missing out on all future employer contributions, forgoing the security of guaranteed benefits, and the freedom to lose half of your Pension fund next time the stock market took a dive.

Understandably the enthusiasm for these new-found freedoms soon began to diminish and it became apparent that someone was responsible for literally millions of people losing valuable Pension benefits. Of course, the Government had no reason to take responsibility; they had only passed the legislation permitting it to happen in the first place and ran TV ads actively encouraging it, so they certainly couldn't be held responsible. No, it must be those bad old insurance Companies, who strangely for commercial business were seeking to increase their customer base and profits.

The Financial Services Authority cried foul and ordered a full review of every single Pension transfer case. This started in 1994 and took 8 years to complete with more than 1.7 million people having their transfers reviewed. Disregarding the time and effort required to review each case, some of which took hundreds of hours and several years to resolve, it resulted in £11.8 billion being paid in compensation for those who had been 'mis-sold' as the expression came to be known, and disciplinary action being taken against more than 300 firms. A good example of financial regulation in action perhaps but what's that got to do with you?

The effects of this very expensive and time-consuming exercise have been long lasting and are still being felt in the Pension transfer arena today. There were some positive outcomes for consumers in that anyone advising on Pension transfers now has to be suitably qualified and there are strict procedures laid down by the FSA when conducting Pension transfer advice. Transfers are, however, still considered very much a high-risk transaction and only the bravest of Advisory gladiators willing to walk into the Pensions transfers arena will be able to offer you this service. Of the 30,000+ Advisers currently practicing in the UK only 10,000 are actually qualified to advise on Pension transfers, of which only 4,000 actually chose to be authorized by the FSA to do so, so it's very much a specialist sport.

Many institutions prefer not to get involved at all, the Banks seem particularly adverse to this kind of advice, preferring to tell their customers it can't be done, rather than it won't be done. Similarly, many large firms of IFAs have a 'No Transfer Advice' policy and quite frankly I don't blame them, it is tantamount to putting a ticking time bomb in your filing cabinet.

Pension transfer advice involves making predictions about the future and unless you are a client of Nostradamus Financial Planning this will involve lot of educated guesswork, or to give it its Sunday name 'calculated assumptions' which is really just guesswork in a dinner jacket.

If any one of the 'calculated assumptions' turns out to be wrong, and the Law of Sod suggests that a lot of them will be, then the financial rationale for transfer may well also turn out to be wrong, leaving the transferee (that's you!) out of pocket and the poor fool who recommended the transfer (that's me!) liable to claims for compensation, and as Pension transfers are not protected by the Statute of Limitations this means that the risk of claim for compensation exists for as long as you do. You can therefore be sure that any IFA reviewing your Pensions with a view to transfer will be an experienced specialist who takes the job very seriously.

Freedom?

If Pension transfers are so fraught with danger for all parties why would anyone wish to even consider transferring away from their safe and warm Company Pension Scheme? There are a variety of reasons and every one will be different but 'choice' and 'flexibility' are the 2 words that come up more and more in conversations about Pension transfers. As in so many aspects of our lives we all want ever-more choice as to how we spend our lives and this is never more apparent than in respect of Company Pensions. Gone are the days when everyone was happy to sit watching the clock tick until their 65th birthday then on the anointed day accept their Pension and lump sum in a particular format and remain in receipt of that Pension for the rest of their natural.

Whether it is choice to invest where you want, retire when you want, take partial retirement, take only a proportion of your Pension or just take your tax-free cash and keep on working, the motive of freedom to choose is a strong one.

Who's solvent now?

An emergent reason for people wishing to transfer is the massive financial uncertainty surrounding Company Pension Schemes, with more and more schemes closing, deficits, Company bankruptcies and applications to join the Pension Protection Fund there is a genuine fear amongst scheme members that their scheme will not be around to honour its obligations and pay them when they reach retirement age.

For many people this has been a fear that has come true – just ask the 65,000 people that are claiming their Pensions from the Government-sponsored Financial Assistance Scheme as a result of their former employers failing between 1997 and 2005, or the

200,000 members of schemes currently in assessment by the Pension Protection Fund.

This is a risk that as a Pensions Adviser it is difficult to quantify, chances are you will have local knowledge about your scheme, contacts and experience that will put you in a better position to judge the long-term prospects for your former employer than I will by reading the Company accounts that are probably 18 months out of date anyway.

The view held by many in this situation is a simple one; a Pension bird in the hand is preferable to an unknown amount in the Pension bush at age 65. This tends to be a decision made on emotion rather than hard financial facts. I have often had to point out to people that as a result of transferring their Pension their income could be only 50% of what it would be if they remained in their Company Scheme until 65. This is still not necessarily a deterrent and I am often countered with the point 'better 50% of something...' so if you are one of those people who with the cold hard facts in front of them are still prepared to take a 50% drop in income, please consider the following:

The case for the defence

Your Pension may seem like something way off in the future with an almost unreal quality giving you a sense of 'what you've never had you won't miss.' This is not the case, Pensions are deferred salary and may provide you with an income for 30 years or more, are you sure you want to gamble with that amount of money?

Constant publicity about deficits which are usually very scary numbers with lots of zeros on the end need to be placed in perspective. What is the amount as a percentage of the total liabilities of your scheme? How many years will it take to rectify? What is it in relation to the Company's profits or turnover? What sort of improvement is required for investment returns to squash this deficit? How much does the fund need to grow to bring your scheme back into balance?

These are all questions to consider before you seriously start looking at a transfer as an option on solvency grounds.

The number of active members, that is those actually contributing into the scheme, can seem small compared to those members who are in receipt of their Pensions or are deferred members (those who have left but are still entitled to Pensions from the scheme in the future), but this is true for the majority of schemes and does not in itself sound the death knell of the scheme.

If the scheme is closed to new members or has closed completely then those running the scheme are in a position to quantify, to a large degree, the extent of their future financial liability and have an idea how much money they are going to need to pay every member's Pension so they can manage the scheme accordingly, this greatly reduces the chances of the scheme becoming insolvent.

When you begin to consider these issues in tandem with the figures, the situation for your scheme may not be quite as devastating as might first appear and while emotion will always play a part in your decision to transfer, make sure you have examined all of the facts before reaching your judgement.

Enhanced Transfer Values – If it looks too good to be true...

This is another wonderful piece of Pensions industry creativity, in simple terms an Enhanced Transfer Value is a bribe, the polite amongst us may say that it makes sound commercial sense for all parties and that it is best described as an incentive, personally I think we all know where we are if we stick to calling it a bribe.

In a bid to reduce their liabilities, a number of Pension schemes are offering financial incentives for members to leave their Pension Scheme. This means they can then wash their hands of you and gives the scheme one less member to worry about providing for in retirement.

Enhanced Transfer Values take two forms, the offer of a larger transfer value which could be enhanced by as much as 30%, so it's an attractive offer, or a cash sum payable directly to you (subject to NI and Income Tax of course) when you transfer away from the scheme. This very generous offer from your former employer will usually arrive with a fairly tight time limit so you have to make up your mind sharpish for what is promoted as a once in a lifetime offer, which it may well turn out to be. Won't you kick yourself if you turn it down and then the scheme becomes insolvent?

Of course you will but this still needs to be placed in context. Whilst this offer may indeed be attractive I would NOT use it as a basis for deciding whether or not to transfer from your scheme, in fact I would, as far as possible, completely disregard this figure when reaching your decision as to whether to transfer or not. Absolutely discount the cash offer unless you are really desperate, the Income Tax and NI take the shine off that, after the Government have taken their third what are you really getting?

For a simple comparison calculate the offered cash enhancement as a percentage of your annual Pension income, think of it as an advance payment, so if after NI and tax your enhanced offer will be £2,000 and your annual Pension is currently worth £12,000 per annum you are being offered a bribe, sorry, *incentive*, of 2 months' Pension payments in return for forgoing all of your guaranteed benefits for 30 years or more?? Doesn't seem quite so attractive now does it?

Taking the bribe as a part of a larger transfer value is certainly the preferred option and to calculate the benefit of this route ask your Adviser to run a parallel analysis, you will then be able to see in very simple terms what is really on offer.

If you receive a letter basically saying "Would you like £2,000 for free?" who would not be tempted, but they know that - that's why they're doing it! Please put the offer into context, it might be a good deal for you, but then again...

Pension Increase Conversion Option

This is another exercise in reducing Pension costs by reducing exposure to inflation and longevity risk. It can be offered to existing Pensioners or built in as an option for deferred members at retirement. The deal is that in exchange for giving up future Pension increases – typically those accrued before April 1997, you get a higher non increasing Pension in return. This means you, the member, carry the inflation risk rather than the scheme, ITV are one of the better-known Companies to undertake this exercise, you could say they've given themselves a commercial break. Once again it is a case of carefully calculating what is being given up, rather than what is being gained, because as with Enhanced Transfer Values, remember who the real winner of this offer is intended to be.

How can a Pension Transfer Analysis help me reach a decision?

A Transfer Analysis will make a direct comparison between remaining a scheme member until retirement age and the benefits of placing your transfer value (the monetary amount your former employer's Pension Scheme calculates your Pension benefits to be worth) into a Personal Pension then purchasing an Annuity at Scheme retirement age.

We make these comparisons in the interests of producing a comparable situation for your consideration as both your Company Scheme and an Annuity offer a secured Pension for life. However, the assumptions used in arriving at the comparison are just that, as we can only estimate future levels of inflation, investment returns, Annuity rates and so forth. The figures arrived at are not an exact prediction, merely an indication of what you might receive at retirement.

A Transfer Analysis Report provides you with a snapshot of the value of the Pension benefits you currently have compared with a Personal Pension. Your transfer value invested in a Personal Pension will need to achieve a certain rate of return each year to match the benefits within your existing scheme. This rate of return is usually expressed as a percentage and described as the 'Critical Yield', but recent changes have meant that it is not quite as critical as it used to be.

Critical Yield is based on the annual rate of growth your transfer value would need to achieve to purchase an Annuity and provide you with the income and other benefits, such as index linking, Spouse's Pension etc, that you would be giving up from your previous employer's Pension Scheme. As we shall see, more and more people are choosing other income options than an Annuity, so the comparison may provide a benchmark comparison but in many instances it will be of limited use.

The larger the Critical Yield, the higher the rates of growth required to match your existing scheme's benefits and if you anticipate taking the benefits before normal retirement age, the Critical Yield will be even higher because your transfer value has a steeper investment hill to climb in a shorter time.

The Critical Yield relates not only to the actual Pension to be paid, it also takes into account any additional benefits provided by your Pension Scheme such as Spouse's or dependents' benefits both before and after retirement, index linking or a lump sum payable on death. The actual percentage rate quoted in your Transfer Analysis report will therefore reflect the cost of providing these benefits as well as a Pension income in retirement. Within a Personal Pension environment these additional benefits would all have to be paid for separately and could add substantially to your retirement planning costs.

Depending on your personal circumstances these ancillary benefits may not be important to you, for example you don't need a Spouse's Pension if you are single or children's benefits if they are grown up, but we must take them into account during our analysis of your scheme.

The higher the Critical Yield figure required, the less likely it is that a transfer to a Personal Pension would be beneficial for you, when considering the financial situation alone. It is difficult to definitively say if the Critical Yield could be achieved but as Personal Pension providers are obliged to illustrate Pensions using growth rates of between 5%-9%, I would suggest anything above that level would be very difficult to achieve, not least without a substantial degree of investment risk.

If, for example, we conduct our analysis and conclude that the Critical Yield is 2% per annum, you could consider transferring in the knowledge that you would not have to take an undue level of risk to match the benefits from your scheme at retirement age. If, on the other hand, we conclude that your Critical Yield is 9% that is going to be very, very difficult to achieve. If the Critical Yield is 16% the chances of achieving 16% each and every year between now and your retirement are virtually nil so you will transfer in the full knowledge that there is every possibility you are going to be substantially worse off at retirement. How do these figures actually translate into the real world of investment returns?

To provide you with an indication of what your fund would need to achieve in the real investment world in relation to the Critical Yield and your attitude to risk, consider the following returns for different investment sectors running from 1st January to 31st December over recent years. The table illustrates average annual returns from different investment classes listed in descending order of perceived risk i.e. Global Equities are high risk, Money Market is low risk.

Yearly Returns by sector

Name	2006	2007	2008	2009	2010
Sector Average: Global Equities	7.5%	9.5%	-24.1%	24.4%	15.8%
Sector Average: UK All Companies	16.8%	2.4%	-31.7%	29.6%	17.5%
Sector Average: UK Direct Property	15.9%	-12.2%	-19.8%	-0.2%	10.7%
Sector Average: Sterling Corporate Bond	0.6%	0.7%	-10.9%	17.8%	8.8%
Sector Average: Money Market	3.8%	4.7%	4.3%	0.6%	0.2%

Data provided by Financial Express

World Stock markets in the form of Global Equities and UK All Companies were certainly the Sectors to be in during 2009 and 2010, but not so attractive the year before when they retreated by -24.1% and -31.7% respectively, way too risky for those of a nervous disposition. If you want to transfer but you don't want to take huge risks, well why not leave your hard earned cash in a low risk Money Market fund? In 2010 you would have returned a handsome 0.2%. Need I say more?

Of course we are not looking at individual years in isolation and we need to take a longer term view when considering investment until retirement as you may have 5, 10 or 20 years until you want to take your Pension. Now we all know 'past performance is no guide to the future' but I disagree, past performance is the ONLY guide to the future we have to base our investment decisions upon. It may not be a very reliable guide but it is the only one we have and the longer term view we are able to take the greater the chances of our predictions being accurate. We know for instance that over the longer term the stock market will outperform cash and that a spread of investments will provide greater capital security than investing in a single asset.

All investment Advisers will tell you a spread between different types of investments (known as asset allocation) is the cornerstone of any successful investment strategy, but more of that later, so the figures above do not reflect a realistic situation but they do give you an indication of the huge variance in returns between different types of investment assets in recent years which may have been unique, but then again isn't every decade?

What about transferring your benefits to your new or future employer's scheme?

You may be able to transfer your preserved Pension scheme benefits to your current or a future employer's scheme if they are willing to accept transfers. At the current time the majority of schemes are not accepting transfers as it increases their long term financial liability. However, if you are fortunate enough to be working where employees are still welcomed into the Pension scheme that may be a possibility, and if your employer will permit the transfer it is always worth investigating.

Your decision whether or not to transfer will be determined in no small part by the quality of your current scheme compared with the new one and any IFA worth his salt will be able to conduct an analysis to provide you with a recommendation as to whether this is a positive way forward for your retirement plans.

Cheers for Pension Transfers

- ✓ You decide how and when you take your Pension benefits
- ✓ You have choice as to where your funds are invested
- ✓ You have the flexibility to take partial or gradual retirement
- ✓ You break ties with your former employer's Pension Scheme
- ✓ You don't care if your former employer's scheme becomes insolvent
- ✓ You are moving funds to an individual plan under your own control
- ✓ Your tax-free cash may improve after transfer
- ✓ Your Pension income has a chance of improving after transfer
- ✓ You may take your Pension in the format of your choice (for example, take 25% tax-free cash and leave the remainder invested).
- ✓ You have more choices as to how death benefits are paid
- ✓ You have choices whether to include Partner's benefits and at what level
- ✓ You have choices if you elect to purchase an Annuity, for example to protect your income against inflation or make allowance for your Spouse
- ✓ Your income in retirement could be higher if your investments provide returns in excess of the required Critical Yield

Fears for Pension Transfers

- ✗ If you transfer your Pension then income may be lower, perhaps substantially so, as a result of underperforming investments
- ✗ A Pension transfer may involve a level of risk you are uncomfortable with

- ✘ Your Company Pension assures you of a certain level of Pension at retirement regardless of economic or investment conditions
- ✘ Your Pension should be protected by the Pension Protection Fund if your former employer becomes insolvent, this protection will be lost on transfer.
- ✘ Your Pension fund is managed for you, you do not have to concern yourself with the investment or administration of your fund
- ✘ Your benefits between now and retirement may increase in line with inflation to a maximum of 5% per annum
- ✘ At retirement you would receive an income for life which may increase in line with inflation each year, again up to a maximum of 5% per annum
- ✘ If you die in the scheme before retirement your Spouse and/or children may be entitled to a Pension and/or lump sum
- ✘ If your former scheme trustees grant discretionary increases to Pensioners you will not benefit if you transfer away from the scheme
- ✘ Any death benefits, Spouse's or dependents' Pensions will have to be funded separately, these are normally included within your former employer's scheme at no explicit cost to you
- ✘ You may be entitled to less tax-free cash than if you had remained in your former Company Pension Scheme
- ✘ You will be responsible for meeting the costs of administering your Pension fund, these are currently borne by your former employer
- ✘ If you die after retirement in your Company Scheme your Spouse or partner will usually be entitled to an index-linked Pension for the rest of their life

6 Will you marry me?

An Adviser partnership for the longer term

'Will you marry me?' You wouldn't utter those four little words without very careful thought, or at least a few pints, so why do people spend so little time considering what is important to them before choosing a Financial Adviser? Also why is such a comparison relevant?

The relationship with your Adviser should be viewed as a long-term arrangement, indeed it should last longer than the average marriage (only 12 years apparently), it is a union that will have it's ups and downs but generally should be a happy one and the union should bear fruit. Not unimportantly, like marriage, if you make the wrong choice of partner you can end up hurt and angry, not to mention a lot poorer.

For richer or poorer

Financial advice is fast becoming the preserve of the wealthy, whole sections of society simply cannot afford to engage a Financial Adviser to help them. There are numerous reasons for this, not least the reducing number of practicing Advisers and the increasing costs for regulation, compensation schemes to pay for, more support staff needed and less reliance on commissions.

This will become even more pronounced with regulatory changes coming into effect in 2012 which are predicted to reduce Adviser numbers even further. The changes will eliminate commissions completely from investment products, thereby depriving consumers of the choice of paying for advice by way of commission rather than a fee. Levels of qualification required to practice are being raised which should improve the quality of advice but it will certainly drive up the cost. With many fee-based Advisers already charging between £150-£250 per hour it only becomes more difficult for huge parts of that mythical beast known as 'middle England' to engage an Adviser to act for them.

Are rich people rich because they seek financial advice or do they seek financial advice because they are rich? Probably combinations of the two, with huge variations in between. There comes a point where not seeking advice can be detrimental to your financial health and if you can afford to invest in advice there seems little argument for not doing so, but of course I would say that wouldn't I? If you cannot afford to pay an Adviser, or simply don't want to, you do have other choices.

Do-it-yourself financial planning

There is a plethora of information on the internet that should be able to answer most of the questions you will ever have about financial products, tax planning, investment opportunities, fund performance, the stock market and so on. It is almost endless with numerous websites and blogs providing an infinite stream of advice and opinion. Places such as www.thisismoney.com, www.motleyfool.com and www.moneymadeclear.com can help to steer you along the right path. Sites such as www.morningstar.co.uk can give you up-to-the-minute fund information and the likes of www.h-l.co.uk will sell you a Pension or ISA over the net or www.Annuitybureau.co.uk will arrange your Annuity for you with a minimum of fuss.

Information or advice?

These are all useful outlets that do the job as advertised but in most cases they cannot provide you with guidance or advice. They are great sources of information, and that should always be your starting point, but there is a significant difference between information and advice. The financial pages of newspapers are full of topical information recommending strategies to improve your finances and traps to avoid but again this is information rather than advice and does not necessarily fit with your own personal situation. Anyway, if financial journalists know so much how come they still have to work for a living?

Very often people believe that if they gather sufficient information they will be able to make a decision, in effect advise themselves but very often the mouse causes information overload leading to paralysis by analysis. For simple financial planning issues where you have perhaps reached a decision prior to making your investigations this may be so. You have decided to purchase an Annuity with your Pension fund; you just need to decide on what type and what additional benefits you want.

Sites such as www.moneyfacts.co.uk or other best buy tables can provide you with figures, but very often these sites do not cover all of the market so you may be missing out on some of the best rates. The difference may not be a huge amount but it may well allow you to spread the jam from your Pension pot a little more thickly than you otherwise would have done. Significantly these sites can make no recommendation as to the suitability of the product for you and as you will see Annuities can be a lot more complex than they initially appear. A wrong decision now could have a detrimental impact on your income for the rest of your life.

You are at a fork in the road where decisions have to be made and options selected will permanently affect your income so how do you know if you have all the information to make a decision? How do you know if you have the right information? Too much information, as is often the case with the internet, is as confusing as too little. When you do have all the information how do you distil it into a workable financial strategy? How do you decide what parts of the information are critical to your strategy and how do you measure them going forward? How do you prioritise them? Cost them? Can you really be objective about your own financial situation? Do you really want the responsibility?

So why would anyone want to invest in financial advice?

Let's not overlook the huge emotional commitment of managing your own money, by virtue of the blood, sweat and tears you have shed throughout your working life to build it up you cannot be dispassionate or objective about your own investment decisions. Your choices simply cannot be based on cold logic. Emotions will play an even greater role in your planning if your funds begin to fall and the more emotional you become about your financial situation the more subjective your decisions will be.

Real life…

I know this from hard personal experience of managing my own Pension fund. Instead of applying the strict criteria and discipline I apply to my clients' investments I started to get clever, believing I could beat the tried and tested systems I was using to advise my clients. Of course, as markets fell I had to take bigger risks to make up for my losses and naturally these decisions were all backed up by research and proof in my own mind that I knew what I was doing. I could prove to myself it would work, so why didn't it?

With my superior knowledge (otherwise known as an overactive ego!), I had stepped outside the disciplined strategies I applied to my clients' portfolios, but I knew better! After my fund value had fallen off a cliff a few times I decided to start practicing what I preach and applying some objective discipline to my investment strategy. I let someone else take responsibility for the day-to-day investment decisions, a strategy that has paid off not least in terms of returns but also in that I don't spend hours analyzing things to death and worrying about them when I could be doing other things - like sleeping at night!

You could spend all day every day analyzing stock markets and investments and still be no better off than the chap next door that put his money in a Balanced Unit Trust and forgot about it. Men particularly like to be seen to be taking control of their finances and there is something macho about fighting the wild beast of investment markets but it can be very time consuming, emotionally draining and potentially very expensive.

Of course you may enjoy managing your own affairs, for some retired people it becomes a hobby allowing them to stay in touch with the commercial world and keep their grey matter in full working order. There's nothing wrong with that of course, but what if for any reason, be it incapacity or something more permanent, you are no longer able to manage your own affairs or you have responsibility for someone else such as your Spouse? Would they be able to do it for themselves? If not, would they know how to locate someone that could?

It is a perpetual challenge for those of us doing this full time to stay up to date with the constant changes in markets, products, tax law and legislation, not to mention the continual evaluation of risk and portfolios. You are one individual with limited experience against the dark and dangerous investment world. Good luck.

The protective cloak of advice

Electing to invest in financial advice gives you a far greater degree of protection should things turn sour and not go the way you were expecting. By taking advice you are delegating responsibility to a qualified professional who is accountable for the advice performing as you were led to expect, and those expectations will have been confirmed in writing to you at the outset.

If things go wrong, and in the world of financial planning very little can be guaranteed, you at least have someone to turn to, and someone you have paid to account for their recommendations. Investing in advice also provides you with an opportunity to discuss your situation regularly so that you know how your retirement strategy is progressing, be it good, bad or ugly and it will be all of those at some point.

If there is far more bad and ugly than you were expecting and you don't feel that your IFA has performed satisfactorily you can of course complain and IFAs are duty bound to undertake a full investigation into your complaint (even if your complaint is purely verbal) and report back to you in writing with their findings. If you are still dissatisfied you can take your complaint to the Financial or Pensions Ombudsman Service whose decisions are binding on IFAs.

All Advisers are compelled to have Professional Indemnity Insurance to help provide compensation should they be deemed to have given bad advice, this usually provides insurance cover of at least £1m per claim, so again an important additional layer of protection should you choose to invest in advice.

An Equitable lesson

We all remember the Equitable Life fiasco, the consequences of which are still being felt by thousands of Pensioners today. The Equitable, Britain's oldest mutual insurer, with its sanctimonious advertising campaigns, indulged in creative accounting techniques for years. As an investor it seemed an attractive proposition; excellent guarantees from a Company with a pedigree that could win Crufts and to top it all you could deal direct and not have to pay commission to an Adviser, (the fact that the Equitable paid huge bonuses to its sales staff went unremarked).

Equitable simply couldn't balance the books and a House of Lords ruling in July 2000 marked the end of Equitable robbing Peter to pay Paul. The Lords' ruling reinforced the not-exactly-revolutionary idea that Equitable should honour its contractual commitments to policyholders, something it was financially unable to do. I won't bore you with the events of the subsequent 10 years – that would constitute a book in itself – but despite numerous enquiries, committees and reports there are still more than 20,000 policyholders, who, depending upon which report you read, have collectively lost between £3bn-£4bn.

A frustration for some policyholders was that when Equitable went into a tailspin they had nowhere to turn, and I don't just mean someone to complain to or to sue, I mean to fight their corner individually. There have been hundreds of instances over the years where IFAs have picked up the baton to fight insurance Companies on behalf of their clients, not always successfully but remember your IFA is paid by you, so will act for you, not for the insurance Company or investment house.

Could *not* paying for advice actually be more expensive?

Hopefully you can see the point I am making above, you may never be able to quantify what not investing in advice has cost you in the form of regulatory protection, or more importantly by not having a tax-efficient and coherent retirement strategy being managed and monitored regularly by a professional. If nothing else for an ongoing, experienced and objective view of your finances perhaps that Adviser's fee suddenly begins to look like remarkably good value.

Halfway house

Maybe you would like some guidance but don't want the full financial planning experience, a bit of pointing in the right direction is all that you require and you don't feel like you want to get into any long-term relationships with an IFA at this stage. What options do you have?

The internet offers a range of tools to help you determine your requirements, understand your attitude to risk and buy off-the-peg financial solutions such as ISAs and Annuities, you can even write your Will online if you want to. These services are usually known as 'execution only'. You make a specific request for a product or service, no advice or recommendation is involved and the transaction is undertaken on your behalf, very often for investment products that are frequently promoted as 'free'.

Yippee it's free!

You may be assured that they are more likely to be giving away free lunches at the Ritz, than offering 'free' investment products. In the world of investment nothing, and I mean absolutely nothing, is ever free and if you read an advert in the financial section of your Sunday paper or on the internet promoting 'free ISAs' or 'free SIPP' just ask yourself this simple question:

'If this business gives away its products how is it still in business?' Or if that doesn't raise your suspicions ask: 'With all these 'free' investment products I wonder who pays for all those smartly dressed chaps in the City who are earning millions in bonuses and driving Ferraris?'

Believe me there is only one group of people that pays and that is YOU the consumer. As investors have largely wised up to the 'free' ruse, the more popular one now is 'no initial charge' or 'no set-up fee', I am sure both of these claims are absolutely true, so this should then raise the question in your mind, 'So how exactly am I going to be paying for this service?' The answer in the majority of cases will be through the annual management charge on your selected investment funds.

'Free/No set up fee' SIPPs tend to offer a panel of favoured funds in which you may invest and switch between without charge. If you wish to invest in a fund that is not on the panel of favourites then a charge will be applied. The most popular funds tend to be on these panels so investment constraints are not usually an issue for most people, but the annual management charge on these funds can vary significantly.

I have below compared charges on a Portfolio of five well-known funds available through different SIPP providers to illustrate the point. The TER (Total Expense Ratio) is the basic fund charge before the application of any additional charges added by the individual SIPP provider.

Fund Name	% investment Split	Total Expense Ratio	Skandia	Cofunds	Funds Network	Transact	Standard Life
		% per annum	Annual Charge	Annual Charge	Annual Charge	Annual Charge	Annual Charge
Gartmore European Selected Opps	20	1.68	1.79	2.06	2.08	2.14	1.88
M&G Recovery	20	1.65	1.76	2.03	2.05	2.36	1.85
BlackRock Gold & General	20	1.93	2.04	2.31	2.33	2.27	2.15
Fidelity Special Situations	20	1.67	1.78	2.05	2.07	2.38	2.02
Invesco Perpetual High Income	20	1.69	1.8	2.07	2.09	2.15	2.04
Total	100	1.72	1.83	2.10	2.12	2.26	1.99

As you can see from our example if we bought our portfolio independently the annual cost of managing our portfolio would be 1.72%, if we invested via Transact the annual cost would be 2.26%, a difference of 0.54%, a 23% percent difference, every year.

There is also the issue of cash held within a SIPP which has to be retained to pay fees and trade investments. A SIPP should allow investors to choose their own deposit account but some providers won't permit this, insisting cash is held in an account determined by them. They do this so they can then make money by paying you a rate of interest below market rate. Some Companies pay zero interest and don't permit the use of an alternative deposit account while one of the biggest SIPP providers in the UK allows SIPP investors to transfer cash to an account of their choosing - but only after paying charges, including an administration fee of up to £416.

Every SIPP provider is obliged to publish a schedule of fees so cast a discerning eye over these before investing in your 'no charge' SIPP as you may wish to do some sharedealing or other investment activity all of which will come with a fee attached. Some basic shopping around will help you find the SIPP with the most suitable fee schedule for what you are trying to achieve within your portfolio.

So please be wary of SIPPS bearing gifts, one way or another you will pay, and quite rightly. Running an investment for clients is an expensive and time-consuming affair, but the difference in cost can be dramatic, as our example above demonstrates.

If that potential 23% extra annual cost doesn't convince you that 'no set-up fee' may not be a saving after all, take a look at our "effect of charges" box below. A 0.5% higher Annual Management Charge can have a compounding effect of around 5% on your return over a 10 year period. So be wary, it could actually work out cheaper paying a set-up fee or initial charge in return for a lower annual management charge, it all depends on your chosen investment strategy and does of course require some careful comparisons and 'what if?' scenarios to help determine which is the best way forward for you.

The effect of charges

As an example I have applied some very simplistic calculations to a sample portfolio to demonstrate the pernicious effect even a modest hike in charges can have on your portfolio over the longer term. Based on an investment of £100,000 with your fund enjoying headline growth of 7% per annum, and applying no other charges, the approximate fund value at the end of 1, 5, 10 and 20 years for different Annual Management Charges would be as follows:

Annual Management Charge	Fund value after 1 Year	Fund value after 5 Years	Fund value after 10 Years	Fund value after 20 Years
0.5% pa	£106,500	£137,008	£187,713	£352,364
1% pa	£106,000	£133,882	£179,084	£320,713
2% pa	£105,000	£127,628	£162,889	£265,329
2.5% pa	£104,500	£124,618	£155,296	£241,171

Take your partners...

After reading the above you may conclude that rather than spending your retirement huddled over a computer screen analyzing investment funds and charges until you are cross eyed it may be worth exploring the possibility of investing in some Independent Financial advice. The luxury of advice can be considered expensive so you need to decide if you are in a position to pay for it, not only today but over the months and years ahead. Assuming you are prepared to make this long-term financial commitment how do you go about finding a suitable partner, one you can be reasonably satisfied is going to be a permanent part of your life for as long as you need them?

Does size matter?

Every firm is different, there are national organizations employing hundreds of Advisers and support staff right through to specialist boutique operations like ourselves who may appear small but as well as our core team of just four permanent employees, which are the human face of our service, we outsource everything else. This allows us to upsize and downsize when we need to and of course keep our costs to a minimum. We have a team of 32 available that take care of all our Pension Scheme administration, our investment partner that manages many of our client portfolios on a daily basis has a team of 60 analysts and researchers constantly monitoring and managing our clients' portfolios. So our clients have a team of nearly 100 people, dedicated, professional, qualified people, working full time on their behalf. I cannot say we will achieve better results than you but the odds are certainly stacked in our favour. If you choose to work with one of the larger national organizations you will then have potentially hundreds of individuals and huge amounts of resource and experience to call upon.

Continuity of service can be a concern with smaller boutique operations but as well as a disaster recovery plan, in common with all other IFAs, I have to appoint a locum to ensure that if I am abducted by aliens there is someone available to look after my clients, and in turn he has to appoint a locum and so on as a precautionary and very sensible measure to ensure there is always someone in place to take care of my clients should I not be able to do so for any reason. My responsibility does not even end at my own retirement, there has to be a strategy in place to ensure there is continuity of advice and a service available for clients as long as they require it.

The rising demand for the services of boutique style operations seems to be a desire for an individual personal service delivered locally. Our business is based upon relationships as clients want to deal with the same faces year after year, people they get to know and trust. As a society we seem to be shying away from the international conglomerates and multinationals with call centres in foreign parts which repeatedly fail to deliver a reasonable level of service or demonstrate even the most rudimentary levels of customer care or accountability in times of need. Even the high street banks with their emphasis on local contact are continually moving staff around so there is a limited opportunity to build a relationship with an Adviser who may well have moved on by the time of your next annual review.

In these days of uniformity with customer service being turned into a mass-produced and packaged product, clients seem to be prepared to pay a premium for the individual attention they are assured with a boutique size operation. Whatever type of service you are seeking it can be refreshing to find a local specialist that can accommodate and respond to your requirements rather than the other way around as so often seems the case with larger organizations.

Till death us do part

In the same way as when you are looking for any long-term partner you will probably have a wish list. When it came to your Spouse you probably didn't write down a list (although it has been known!), but subconsciously you will have had a list of preferred qualities. As this is a commercial arrangement, you need a list of attributes that you want your financial planning partner to have, and you want to formulate this list prior to meeting any prospective Advisory partners. It could include the following;

1. **Qualifications** There are a whole range of different examinations Financial Advisers can undertake; the pinnacle of academic achievement is that of a Chartered Financial Planner so it is preferable that any IFA you will potentially engage has Chartered status, (not the firm he works for, that is a different thing). Also enquire how long has he been Chartered? The longer the better, as he will be undertaking Continual Professional Development to maintain his or her Chartered status and if nothing else it proves he or she takes their career very seriously as they will probably have spent the best part of 10 years or more studying for exams. Instructing a Chartered Financial Planner may well be more expensive than one that is only qualified to the basic level but it should ensure the quality of the advice and guidance you receive is well beyond the basic level also.

   Whatever field of expertise you are seeking it always makes sense to go for the highest qualified you can afford, and certainly going for the cheapest can prove very costly indeed. I know if ever I am in need of a medical professional I am looking for the highest qualified and most experienced I can find. When choosing a heart surgeon I can't imagine that ensuring he was the cheapest would be the clincher. In fact if he was the cheapest, I would be quite worried. Cheap is good when we are talking tins of beans but when we are talking about something that will affect your whole life and family I don't think cost should be number one on the list of your requirements.

2. **Testimonials** The great difficulty when purchasing any service is how do we know how good the person really is? Is he really worth £300 per hour and how do we judge?

How do we choose a good solicitor or heart surgeon or IFA? Testimonials from existing clients are a great way of finding out about what clients really think about their IFA and very few of us are going to be happy providing a testimonial for someone who we didn't think had done an excellent job for us. So next on your must have list is, 'Can you provide me with testimonials from existing clients (and your mum doesn't count!)?'

Genuine written testimonials should be available for scrutiny in their original form. Simply having on a website, "I am wealthier than I could have ever dreamed," said Mrs S of London doesn't really cut it.

3. **Recommendation** Being referred to an IFA by someone you know and trust is also a very good way to meet a financial planning partner, not least if they don't live up to your expectations you have someone you can go back to and thump! Our own business is a success simply because people refer those they know to us as potential clients, yet there can be reluctance by clients to recommend others in case they cause offence. Surely if you had a choice wouldn't you want those people you cared about looked after by someone you know and trust rather than someone they have picked at random off the internet? Well it probably works the same in reverse so if someone you trust recommends a particular IFA to you it may be well worth putting them on your shortlist.

4. **Are they a retirement planning specialist?** Are they qualified to deal with *all* aspects of retirement planning, Pension transfers, Income Drawdown, Company Schemes etc? You want someone that is doing this full time, not someone that might have been selling life assurance yesterday, medical insurance tomorrow and doing cash flow forecasts on Thursday. Ask the simple question, "Of what percentage of your total number of clients are you currently managing their retirement strategies?"" (Top answer: all of them!)

One of the really useful things about instructing an Adviser is that you will only go through retirement once, your IFA, if you choose the right one, will have been through it hundreds of times and you get to share that wealth of experience, just be sure they have it to share.

5. **Independent?** There are continually changing definitions of what exactly is an Independent Financial Adviser, if they are not independent they may have access only to a limited range of products, services and funds. Many firms claim independence but at the simplest level you want to see their Terms of Business document where it clearly states that they have access to 'whole of market' so they are no way limited in the scope of advice they are able to give you.

   'We are free to choose any investment manager from any fund management firm anywhere in the world' (thank you St James' Place) or 'Through our Pension and investment plans, you can access the investment expertise of a range of industry-renowned fund managers' (thank you Zurich). Nothing wrong with either of these institutions but they are not independent nor do they employ Independent Advisers so make sure you dig deeper than the glossy brochure, so if independence and access to the whole of the market is important to you be sure that your proposed partners are IFA.

   Also you need to check on their 'independent' status, do they offer advice from the full range of investments or are they part of a bigger organization that insists they work from a panel or shortlist? How much independence do they actually have? Are they 'authorised and regulated by the FSA' or 'appointed representatives of xyz Limited'? Are policy decisions made by the person sitting in front of you or are they told what to do by someone higher up the food chain?

Is your IFA a shareholder or partner in the firm, or is he an employee? This will help you determine how much independence and autonomy he or she actually has. Most of the time this may not be important but in times of crisis, and you can be sure there will be some along the way, you need someone who can exercise independence of thought and spirit and has the latitude to make decisions quickly without the need to refer up the management hierarchy.

This point also helps to explain the growing popularity of financial planning boutiques, small IFA businesses with only one or two IFAs offering a highly bespoke and individual investment advisory service to a very limited number of clients. With the ever-increasing pace of world economies, the ability to adapt and respond quickly to changing circumstances is vital and the level of independence your Adviser enjoys will be a key determinant of that ability.

6. **How does your Adviser get paid for his service?** All firms offering financial advice can provide you with a fees menu. The snappy official name for this document is 'key facts about the costs of our service' and it will detail the various fees that your proposed IFA will levy for their products and services. These can usually be downloaded (for example from www.pensionmatters.net if you're interested!). Fees are now the preferred method as commissions paid on investment products are going to be outlawed in 2012. Fees can take various forms; payable either by the hour, initial plan fee + retainer, or more often as a percentage of your investments, for example a charge of 3% of the amount invested and anything from 0.5% - 2% per annum for looking after your portfolio.

Real life...

If you make an investment with Fidelity into your ISA at www.fidelity.co.uk you pay £10,000 and they invest £10,000 for you. If the same transaction is undertaken for you on the advice of an IFA there will be a charge levied for the advice, either an invoice for perhaps £300 or as is more often the case, a percentage deducted from your investment of anything from 1%-5%. Typically the fee is 3%; so you have invested £9,700 in your ISA and invested £300 in financial advice.

Paying for advice. Ouch!

The initial plan and retainer method is an increasingly popular system employing state-of-the-art software and cash-flow modelling programmes to consider every aspect of your life and put together a comprehensive financial plan, covering every eventuality. The cost of your plan can vary from £500 to £20,000 depending upon the level of complexity. Thereafter you may well pay a fee for the implementation stage, such as the purchase of investments and Pensions, or the drawing up of Wills and Trusts. Then you may pay a retainer to your IFA of £200 per month for example so that you can sit and review your plan on a regular basis to ensure that you end up with a future something like the one you imagined.

Many professional firms still operate on an hourly fee basis, although this appears to be changing and that in my view is good news. The reason for charging by the hour dates back to the 16th century, when the 'modern' quill pen was designed. As writers could only write so fast, hence, work was charged based upon the time it took to write.

IN ACCORDANCE WITH
IFA GUIDELINES I'M MAKING
OUR RUMUNERATION STRUCTURE
FAR MORE TRANSPARENT

Today, this charging structure is totally outdated. The time that it takes someone to do something has nothing to do with the value that it creates. I want a bad tooth extracted as quickly and as painlessly as possible, I don't care how much time the dentist spends preparing for the job! Is a car that takes 2 days to build any better than one that is built in a day or is the production line just more efficient? The editor of this book was paid per thousand words to edit, if she had been paid by the hour she would probably still be reading it!

If someone is charging you by the hour there is no incentive to complete a task quickly. There is a benefit to them of working more slowly; you carry all the risk as you do not know how large your bills will be so the cost is unquantifiable. Also who wants to be receiving invoices every quarter? The administration of this type of system only adds to the cost, cost that is ultimately borne by you the client and because the system is so opaque it is open to all sorts of abuses.

Personally I prefer the percentage method, any Pension investment you have made has received tax relief so the taxman is making a contribution to your fee, and if you are transferring from one Pension to another your fund will hopefully have benefited from some tax-free growth along the way, reducing the net cost to you even further. I am quite happy to take a cheque for my fee but why give me a cheque out of your bank account on funds that have already been subject to income tax and National Insurance?

Real life…

You wish to invest £20,000 into retirement planning, 97% of it will be invested in a Pension and 3% of it will be invested in advice from me. So how would you like to pay the £600 advice fee? You could authorise me to deduct it from your Pension fund on day one, quick, simple and after basic rate tax relief it has only cost you £480. Or I could raise an invoice and you then send me a cheque, that way the whole £20,000 is invested in your Pension plan. However, assuming you are employed my £600 fee will be paid after deduction of tax at 20% and NationalInsurance at 11% so it will actually cost you around £832 plus VAT. See why I'm a Financial Adviser?

With regard to ongoing fees for managing your portfolio these vary enormously and should be considered in conjunction with the service package on offer, only you can decide if they offer good value for money. The value of the work should be relative to the amount of capital you have and our own fee scale is very much performance related. We believe it is fair for us to be rewarded at a higher level for generating £10,000 rather than £10. It also means that our fortunes are aligned with yours as our income only increases if your fund value increases. Equally if your funds fall in value so does our income. If we were charging you by the hour we would get paid regardless.

If the standard fee charged by your IFA is 1% per annum, is he or she clearly adding value of at least 1%? Is the investment management generating 1% above what you could have reasonably expected? Do the additional services such as regular valuations, meetings, reports and additional services such as Wills and Trust planning justify the performance-related 1% each and every year? Ask for a copy of their Client Service Charter or Wealth Management Agreement so you have in black and white exactly what you do and don't get for your money.

This is particularly important when you are paying by retainer as the fee has no relation to how your investments perform, your IFA gets paid regardless, which is fine as long as the range of services you are being provided with justify that Direct Debit getting actioned every month. I look at some of the Wealth Management Agreements on offer and they are extremely comprehensive, but will you actually use those services? Do you really need a 24-hour investment helpline? Do you really want to sit down with your IFA every 3 months to review your portfolio or have your Will and Trusts reviewed every year? You might, but then again...

It sounds obvious but make sure you read the Terms of Business and any management agreement very carefully before signing. Not least if you do sign up with a particular IFA and for whatever reason they prove big on promises and short on delivery, what is the notice period? Are there any barriers that will stop you moving your portfolio elsewhere quickly and cheaply?

Obtain a copy of their Investment Policy Statement

As we will look at in a later chapter, there are numerous different investment strategies and lots of competing arguments as to why one investment philosophy is superior to another. IFAs spend many hours debating the merits of different strategies, but what is important is that your potential IFA *has* a strategy. If they tell you, "We research the market at the appropriate time, apply certain criteria and make recommendations on that basis," that is not a strategy, that is a wing and a prayer investment management.

You want to be sure that they have thought long and hard about their investment proposition, how and why they have arrived at their conclusions, what exactly is on offer and how it will work for you in practice. Are they managing your money themselves or has that been delegated to someone else and in both cases why is that? What measurements or benchmarks are they applying to monitor their system and what can you expect from it in terms of returns and costs?

Also do you have any special investment requirements on religious or ethical grounds and how will their investment proposition meet your requirements?

All these questions should be answered in the IFA's investment brochure or on their website. You need to look beyond the colourful graphs and pie charts; it is the philosophy you need to be comfortable with. If you don't feel comfortable with their investment offering, then don't even bother considering them as a partner. Even if they tick all of your other boxes many times over, you will never be at ease dealing with them.

The man with two dentists ends up with no teeth

Should you use more than one Adviser? One of the first tasks your appointed IFA will undertake is a review of all of your Pensions and investments and prepare a schedule so that you can see exactly your financial position and he can then begin plotting a course for your retirement. Without access to all of the information and control of all the assets involved it makes the job extremely difficult. Plotting the course with only half the coordinates makes your voyage arduous to plan and you will forever have to make radical changes as new information comes to light.

You may, for example, have enjoyed a long relationship with your Accountant who previously made various financial arrangements for you and you are reluctant to leave him as you have always valued his opinion. Unfortunately, you need to make hard choices.

Personally, I would refuse to work with a client unless I had access to all of their information exclusively, without which it makes proper financial planning virtually impossible. I have had put to me in the past such arguments as the value of a second opinion, the opportunity to negotiate better fees, and spreading eggs between baskets, all of which may carry a certain validity but all of these points are undermined if your Adviser is unable to formulate a coherent investment strategy. It will lead to confusion for both parties, increased costs and missed opportunities, not to mention making things more complex at a time when simplicity is one of the keys to success.

There is also the underlying psychological effects that if you are not 100% committed to your Adviser he is not going to be 100% committed to you, and whilst no IFA is going to admit this out loud believe me it's true. If he has work to do for two clients, one of which he has 100% responsibility for their affairs and one he is only partially involved with, who is going to take priority? Every time?

If you feel unsure about making such a commitment to an Adviser then maybe there are other factors at work, even sub-consciously, that you should address, there is no room for three people in this marriage, it has to be based on openness, trust and most of all commitment.

That's the easy bit done – now on to your shortlist!

OK so you've applied all your criteria, you know you are looking for a Chartered Financial Planner with at least 10 years' experience, Pensions qualified with a working day-to-day knowledge of the retirement market. Where do you go about finding those individuals?

You could do worse than start at www.unbiased.co.uk which is a nationwide database of IFAs. You can filter by postcode, which raises another important and maybe obvious point, I always think it is useful to have someone local to where you live or work, because I have found in my own experience that long-distance relationships do not tend to work as well.

You can of course type keywords into Google, which again should bring you some local Advisers who may meet your very strict requirements, and a bit of website research is a good way of eliminating those that don't. The best way is to ask someone you trust if they could refer you, then you are assured of a certain level of service as the IFA has the added incentive that he or she wants to do a good job to please his existing client.

The aim of this exercise is to arrive at a shortlist of IFAs who you plan to interview for their suitability, and believe me this is very much a two-way street. The IFA will also be interviewing you for suitability and how you are going to fit into his practice. This is a good thing because, like any relationship, for it to succeed both parties have to be happy. Ever-increasing costs means that the days when IFAs would take on any client with a pulse are long gone, they are increasingly discriminatory; there is no benefit for them to be taking on client that doesn't fit their business model, so you will soon get the message if you are not right for them, just as if they are not right for you.

The interview stage is far and away the most challenging part of the process, and unless you take an instant dislike to the first IFA you may well sign on the dotted line. This is like marrying your first girlfriend; it seems a fantastic idea at the time but years later the idea seems totally ridiculous, so why does it happen with IFAs?

The reason is simple, you will probably like him or her and more than likely they will like you too, so why bother shopping around? All IFAs love meeting people, for me it's the best part of the job, everyday there are new people coming into my life telling me all sorts of things about their jobs and their families and their lives. It is never dull, it helps satisfy my innate curiosity about the human condition and I have an endless supply of anecdotes to entertain with when I get home at night. Over the years clients will share the trials and triumphs of marriage and children, business won and lost, markets crashed and cars smashed, holidays from heaven and neighbours from hell, even occasionally we will talk about financial matters.

This all stems from that fateful initial meeting when most people decide, maybe even on a subconscious level, this is a guy I can talk to, I like him. This is no conjuring trick because the chances are he will like you too and subconsciously have decided he wants to work with you. Somewhere on a deeper level some bridge of trust is slowly being constructed that once built there seems little need to go anywhere else. Believe me you should, if for no other reason than to confirm that the first person you met is definitely the right one for you. Very often prospective clients will arrive at our office for the first time almost under sufferance as their meeting has been recommended by someone they know and they have only really come along as a courtesy to that person, firmly of the belief that we won't be able to help them with, "I've already made my mind up" or in a recent example, "I don't really know what it is but I don't want it". (You can guess what happened next!) If I genuinely believed a person's visit would be a waste of time I wouldn't invite them in, because then it is also a waste of my time and money. If nothing else meeting Advisers gives you the opportunity to consider a different perspective and perhaps hear some new ideas – unless of course you already know everything! Don't forget you only experience retirement once – I've been through it hundreds of times.

As I have said more than once, this relationship could last longer than the average marriage; you need to be as sure as you can be that this is a relationship that is going to work. If you have a Spouse or partner makes sure he or she is with you and ask as many difficult questions as you can. Ask about timescales for various jobs, meet the staff you will deal with, and always, always go to their office as this will tell you a lot about how they work and give you the opportunity to look under the bonnet of the operation.

Human chemistry being what it is, there are people you are going to meet and not like, even if you can't determine actually why, and the interview process will help you identify this minority. It is extremely important that you are comfortable with whom you are proposing to work with and spending an hour of your time is a worthy first investment in the advice process. Most IFAs are happy to offer you an initial consultation without charging for their time so take full advantage of that.

After you have completed your interviews it is decision time and based on the premise that they wouldn't have even made the interview if they couldn't do the job, it is down to a matter of who you felt you would be happiest spending time with over the coming years and this could also involve factors such as location and office staff as well as the qualities of the Individual Adviser.

What happens next?

Once you have agreed upon terms with your chosen Adviser they will ask you to sign a Letter of Authority which will allow them to contact all of your existing Pension providers and investment Companies so that they can begin to formulate a schedule of your existing arrangements. This could take up to 3 months as Companies are notoriously slow in responding to requests for information, another reason to establish a relationship with an Adviser well before you are actually going to need them!

Once your IFA has established exactly what you have financially, you can then jointly consider your 'me plc' accounts and your attitude to risk, goals and aspirations. Your IFA will then begin putting together some recommendations in the form of a plan, looking at some of the options as to how and where to generate your retirement income and how his financial recommendations will meet your life goals.

These should demonstrate various possible future outcomes, perhaps not all of them positive but hopefully all of them realistic. You can then look forward free from worry, with confidence that your financial affairs now have a written strategy that you can refer to as a template. When you have agreed your strategy your IFA will begin the implementation stage, which is making the necessary investments, constructing your investment portfolio, instructing Wills and Trusts, opening accounts and so on.

It is these options that we are going to look at in more detail in the coming chapters so you can begin to understand what choices you have as you approach retirement. If you can afford to pay for an Adviser partner to help you make those choices all the better for you.

Hopefully this chapter has offered some guidance before you make that commitment to your new Advisory partner and it is no accident that this chapter is one of the longest in this book. The decisions you make when choosing an Adviser can have a major impact on your financial wellbeing and that of those around you, so you need to be confident you have made an informed and rational choice. Choosing the right Adviser as the right strategic partner is not only important, it can enhance your retirement in ways you don't even know exist. Happy hunting!

7 Learning to expect the unexpected

Managing Investment Risk

When you lay your head on your pillow at night and sleep gently suffocates your fading thoughts, the last thing you want passing through your mind is concerns about money and investment risk. Whatever you decide to do with your retirement funds, the chances are that some or all of your hard-earned cash is going to be invested in some form. You may be hugely experienced in investments – owning shares, funding ISAs, Unit Trusts and Pension funds – or you may have no experience at all.

Regardless of your level of investment knowledge or experience this chapter is designed to give you an overview of the different types of risk you may face, explain some of the terminology used and help you gain a deeper insight into your own attitude to risk. There is never a right or wrong way for you regarding investment risk, there is only the best way. Only if you have the gift of clairvoyance will you know if you are right. If you haven't the gift then like the rest of us you will have to use the resources, both intellectual and physical, that you have available to make an informed decision and keep your mind open enough to review and modify those decisions as events sculpt your investment experience.

What do we mean by risk? Our generation is no stranger to risk, as children we rode around in cars without seatbelts. In the front. If we wanted to go on a bike ride we didn't put on helmets and reflective clothing, we simply got on our bikes and took off in the spirit of *Easy Rider*, so don't talk to our generation about taking risks.

More seriously, never has there been a more misunderstood and difficult-to-determine concept than risk in the world of investment. First we need to understand what we mean by risk in those terms, be clear how we measure it and then appreciate how we can factor it into our investment strategy to work for us rather than against us.

One polite definition of risk is "accepting the possibility that an investment's actual return may be different than expected." This includes the possibility of losing some or all of the capital you invested. Do not disregard the importance of this last sentence. I repeat: This includes the possibility of losing some or all of the capital you invested.

Investment Companies and Advisers allocate huge amounts of time and money to developing risk assessment and risk management strategies to help investors, a key component of which is the client risk profiling tool which seeks to determine your attitude to, and quantify your appetite for, investment risk. These come in various forms of questionnaire and are growing increasingly sophisticated, applying psychometric profiling techniques in an attempt to produce a concise definition of your personal risk profile.

As it is so difficult to quantify and articulate investment risk it has resulted in huge problems for investors and Advisers alike. One of the biggest areas of investor complaints is that they were advised to invest in something that was not commensurate with their risk profile, this is usually expressed more bluntly - their investment has fallen in value and they weren't expecting it.

Risk and return – as inseparable as night and day

A fundamental concept in investing is the relationship between risk and return. The greater the amount of risk that you as an investor are willing to accept, the greater the potential return. The reason for this is simple; investors need to be compensated financially for taking additional risk with their capital.

A Government Bond, known as a Gilt, is considered to be one of the safest investments and, when compared to a Bond issued by a PLC, provides a lower rate of return. The reason for this is that a PLC is more likely to go bankrupt than the UK Government. As the risk of investing in a Corporate Bond is higher, investors are offered a potentially higher rate of return. Investing in shares is higher risk again, so the rewards reflect that, a return known as the 'equity risk premium.' The Barclays Equity Gilt Study which has been published continuously since 1956 has repeatedly demonstrated that the equity risk premium produces a return of in the region of 4% per year above what you would have received if you had invested in Gilts, and so it is up and down the risk scale.

To demonstrate this on a global scale consider the risk premium assumptions of different markets below, the further to the right you move along the scale the greater the volatility and risk, and therefore the greater the potential return.

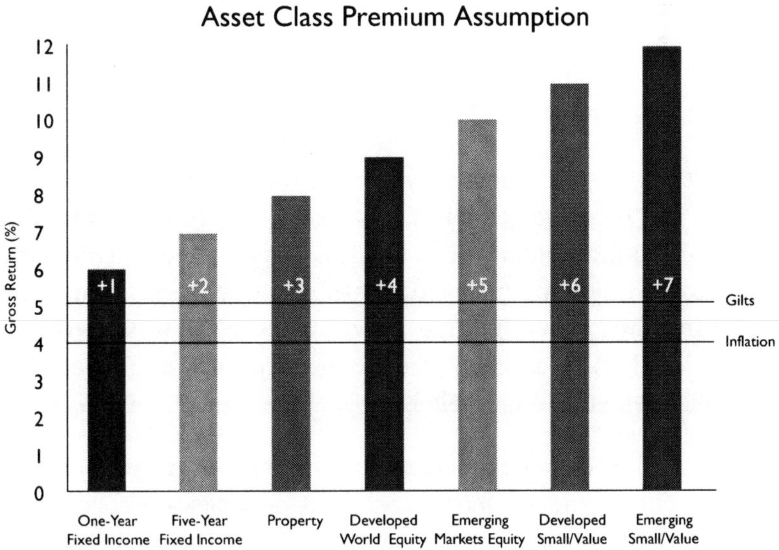

(Dimensional Fund Advisors)

As an investor you never disregard the very definite relationship between return and risk. Put simply; to generate return over time you have to accept risk. Looking back at our table in Chapter 6 showing annual returns for different sectors you can clearly see that lower risk investments generally produce the lower returns. It is no coincidence that those at the bottom of the table in terms of return are also at the bottom of the risk scale.

If all you require to meet your retirement and investment goals is a return of 2% per year then you need venture no further than National Savings and Investments, if you require a 10% return then we are definitely swimming in shark-infested waters. Not a problem if you are fully prepared and ready for those risks, the difficulty arises all too often when you need a 10% return but only want a 2% risk.

Whatever you decide upon will incur risk, even if you leave your money in the bank there is the risk that the value of your funds are being eaten by inflation, even in times of low inflation. Or, as we have seen more recently, the very real risk that the bank will no longer be there! Before we look at the different types of risk let us briefly consider what general protection you have as a UK investor.

Investor protection

There is a mass of different types of investor protection within the UK and over the years it has played a vital role in protecting savers and policyholders alike, but it is not all-encompassing and never for a single moment enter into an investment of any kind under the illusion that if things go wrong there will be someone or something there to come to your rescue in your hour of need. Just ask policyholders of Equitable Life.

With regard to the current regulatory investor protection regime, should your provider become insolvent deposits are covered up to £85,000 per institution and most types of investment business are also covered up to a maximum limit of £50,000 with insurance advising covered for 90% of the claim, without any upper limit. Further information about compensation scheme arrangements is available from the Financial Services Compensation Scheme at www.fscs.org.uk.

What investor protection is not designed to do is protect you from the consequences of your own decisions, although it frequently does. Investors occasionally suffer from memory lapses and are convinced they were never explained the risks involved or the fact that they could lose money. In fact they were assured of a guaranteed return! All of which may be true but it is becoming increasingly difficult for investors to rely on this scenario as Advisers and fund managers document in great detail so much of what they have recommended to you in what is called a Suitability Report.

As well as demonstrating suitability a report should, along with any associated documentation, confirm all the terms and conditions, costs, risks, options, timescales etc. In short it should answer all the questions you have and maybe even answer some you didn't even know you had. Your Adviser may ask you to sign your Suitability Report to confirm receipt so please make sure you read it. From cover to cover.

After investing you have up to 30 days from the day your investment is made in which to change your mind. The recipient of your funds will send you a 'Cancellation Notice' the clue is in the name, all you have to do is sign it, send it back and bingo! The investment fairy magics your money back from whence it came and makes it all seem just like a bad dream. As you have a whole month to muse and meditate, cogitate and consider, review and reflect there is no way you should end up with anything other than what you expected.

The end of capitalism (well almost!)

The question as to whether your money is safe has been asked with a tad more poignancy since the dark days of 2008 which saw some slightly unusual happenings in the world of finance. Queues outside every branch of Northern Rock was the first bemusing sign of the impending financial meltdown that saw so many familiar institutions on the brink of collapse: Royal Bank of Scotland, Halifax, Bradford & Bingley and the Dunfermerline Building Society to name but a few. Institutions we could never have dreamed would collapse in such ignominious circumstances. Thankfully no investors lost as the Government bravely offered to guarantee all investors deposits, even those deposits frozen in Iceland!

Whatever the reasons for the collapse of capitalism, we can look at how many life insurance Companies or retail investment houses went with the begging bowl looking for bailouts from the taxpayer. I am glad to say the grand total of none. This is no reason to be smug but if those institutions can withstand a financial hurricane of such force and still be standing it gives me some comfort that they must be in pretty good financial shape, and we would hope a safe home for your money.

Different types of risk

Let's look in more detail at some of the more common types of risk you may encounter along the investment road:

- **Systematic Risk** - influences a large number of assets. A significant political event, for example, could affect several of the assets in your portfolio. It is virtually impossible to protect yourself against this type of risk.

- **Unsystematic Risk** - is sometimes referred to as 'specific risk'. It affects a very small number of assets. For example you own British Airways shares and there is news of a strike by employees. Sound asset allocation will help protect you against unsystemic risk.

  Credit or Default Risk - A Company is unable to pay the contractual interest on its debt obligations. This type of risk is of particular concern to investors who hold Bonds in their portfolios. Bond rating services, such as Moodys, allows investors to determine which Bonds are investment-grade, and which Bonds are kindly classified as junk.

- **Country (or Sovereign) Risk** - A country won't be able to honour its commitments; the recent fears about Greece and Ireland are an example of possible sovereign risk. This can damage the performance of all other financial instruments in that country as well as other countries it has relations with, so-called contagion risk.

- **Foreign-exchange Risk** - When investing in foreign countries you must consider the fact that currency exchange rates can change the price of the asset and any gains could be wiped out by the host currency strengthening against the pound.

- **Interest Rate Risk** - An investment's value will change as a result of a change in interest rates. This risk affects the value of Bonds more directly than stocks.

- **Political Risk** - represents the financial risk that a country's government will suddenly change its policies e.g. raises levels of taxation or devalues it's currency.

- **Market Risk** - This is the most familiar of all risks, otherwise known as volatility, market risk is the the day-to-day fluctuations in an investment's price. Market risk applies mainly to shares but affects all investments to some extent. Volatility is not so much a cause but an effect of certain market forces; it is a measure of risk and the reason why investors can profit. Volatility is essential for returns, but can have a severe detriment upon them. It is this aspect of risk that you really need to fully understand before investing in anything.

What does 'volatility' mean?

We all want the risk that our investments are going to rise in value, it's the risk of a fall in value that causes us problems, and it is this variation, called volatility, which is key to our understanding and acceptance of risk

We're not going to get into anything too technical such as Cokurtosis or Conditional heteroskedasticity (honestly I haven't made those up!) but it is important to understand the fundamentals of how figures that investment professionals throw at you are arrived at as it will allow you to make a more informed judgment and also help you ask some pertinent questions. If you grasp the workings of volatility it will help you appreciate what your investments can do for you, how risk can work to your advantage and realize the limits in respect of what your funds can achieve if they are constrained by fear of risk.

Put simply volatility is a statistical measure of the dispersion of returns for a given investment around the average. The wider the dispersion of returns around the average, the higher the volatility.

Volatility refers to the amount of future uncertainty about the changes in the value of an investment. A higher volatility means that a security's value can potentially be spread out over a larger range, both up and down. A lower volatility means that a security's value does not fluctuate dramatically, but tends to change at a steady pace over a period of time.

Volatility is measured using standard deviation so let's go back to maths class to refresh our memories and we will begin to see how fearsome irrational risk translates into a mathematical concept that we can understand and more importantly measure. We can then take a view, using simple figures, to decide if a particular investment is too risky for you or not risky enough and conclude if it is the right investment for your portfolio.

Standard Deviation

Standard deviation measures how widely the actual return on an investment varies around the average (which is the expected return) year on year. The general principle is simple; the greater the standard deviation around the expected return, the more volatile and hence the more risky an investment is considered. Therefore an investment with year-on-year returns that stay close to the expected (average) return will have a low standard deviation and be considered low risk. Both positive and negative returns contribute equally to our assessment of risk, but it is the negative ones that will potentially cause us sleepless nights.

Risk assessments that rely on standard deviation presume that returns conform to a normal mathematical pattern so that 68% of the time, roughly two years out of every three, returns should fall within one standard deviation and 95% of the time, returns should fall within two standard deviations (often described as the 95% confidence level). This means if our theory holds good we can predict returns 95 years out of every 100 and can be reasonably sure of what to expect in terms of volatility. Let's take a hypothetical example to demonstrate this:

The Steadyaway Fund has an average annual return of 5% with a standard deviation of 1%, we know therefore that 68% of the time returns will fall between 4% and 6% per year (plus or minus one standard deviation) and that 95% of annual returns will fall between plus or minus two standard deviations, which means in 95 years out of 100 returns on the Steadyway Fund should fall between 3%-7% per annum (+/- two standard deviations).

As investors evaluating risk, if we want to invest in the Steadyaway fund we should be prepared to accept this volatility and possibility of a 2% loss in any given year. We could, of course, encounter one of those 5 years out of 100 that produce returns outside our comfort zone but statistically this is unlikely, and it could, of course, just as easily be a swing to the positive side.

If you are feeling more adventurous you could invest in the more volatile Hellforleather Fund which has returned an average of 10% and has a standard deviation of 20%.We can estimate therefore that in 95 years out of 100 returns will swing by as much as -30% to +50% (+/- two standard deviations either side of 10%) so in seeking greater returns we must accept the real possibility of a 30% loss in any given year.

Conclusions about volatility

High volatility can work both for us and against us; it can erode your expected long-term return, but it also provides you with more chances to make big gains. Understanding volatility can be a powerful weapon in our armoury when evaluating risk, either in respect of an individual investment or a proposed portfolio. We still have to decide just how much risk we are prepared to take to achieve our long-term financial objectives.

The sample portfolios below start at the cautious end of the risk/return scale with Portfolio 1 investing in 100% Fixed Interest Stock and no equities. As we gradually move along the scale from Portfolios 1-6 our level of volatility and therefore risk rises as the proportion of equities increases;

Portfolio 1: UK 100% Fixed Interest/0% Equity	**Portfolio 2:** UK 20% Equity/80% Fixed Interest
Portfolio 3: UK 40% Equity/60% Fixed Interest	**Portfolio 4:** UK 60% Equity/40% Fixed Interest
Portfolio 5: UK 80% Equity/20% Fixed Interest	**Portfolio 6:** UK 100% Equity/0% Fixed Interest

Over a period of 21 years our sample portfolios produced a range of returns as follows;

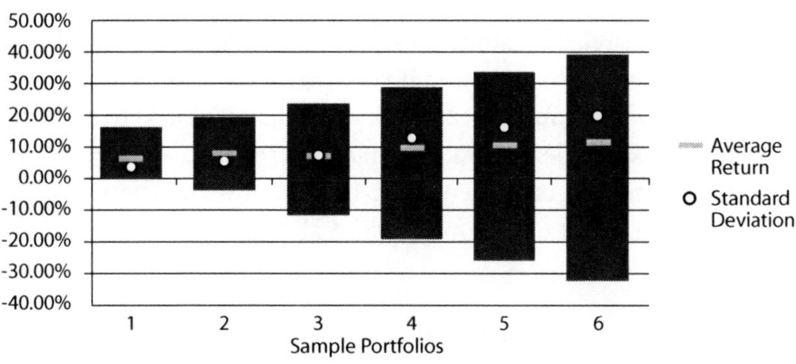

Returns	Portfolio 1	Portfolio 2	Portfolio 3	Portfolio 4	Portfolio 5	Portfolio 6
Highest	15.31%	18.90%	23.49%	28.17%	32.96%	38.58%
Lowest	0.28%	-3.90%	-11.62%	-19%	-26.05%	-32.67%
Average	6.55%	7.41%	8.38%	9.40%	10.48%	11.60%
Standard Deviation	3.58%	5.01%	8.48%	12.35%	16.31%	20.29%

(Dimensional Fund Advisors)

Naturally we are attracted to the high returns of Portfolio 6, of course we would rather have 11.60% every year than the restrained 6.55% of Portfolio 1, but only if we can accept a hit of -32.67% in the middle of that, which would be far from ideal if you were reliant on your portfolio for income.

All volatility needs to be placed in context, and our illustration of sample portfolios provides an indication of the variation in return that can be experienced. If you can only accept volatility +/-5% then Portfolios 1 or 2 are your natural investment habitat, if you are seeking larger returns over the longer term and can accept swings in the value of your investment of +/- 20% then Portfolio 6 may be the place for your funds. Once you have established how much risk you can tolerate and related that to how much return you require to fund your retirement, we then need to start thinking about how exactly we are going to invest your funds.

So where do you sit on the risk scale?

You may have reached some conclusions about your own attitude to risk during this chapter, and if you instruct an Adviser he or she will certainly be asking you some challenging questions to establish a suitable risk profile for you. You may be prepared to take a higher risk with some assets (such as your ISA) than with others (such as your Pension fund) or you may regard all their capital in the same way.

Assume we have investigated your attitude to risk and drawn some conclusions, we have agreed you are a 'Balanced/Medium/Average/Central investor', let's say No 5 on a risk scale of 1-10, so where do we go from here? How do we decide exactly where we are to invest? Should we be considering a blend of fixed interest and stock as in the portfolios above, or should we be looking at more diverse holdings, incorporating property, commodities or timber futures? This is where we need to consider how we allocate your assets to different classes of investment so that we optimize the risk/return balance for you.

I hope you now have a firmer grasp on what you understand about that little word risk, because your understanding of it, and it is very subjective, may actually determine your future happiness. Does that sound too dramatic? Remember it is the spicy invisible ingredient in every investment decision that you will ever make, the silent but permanent partner in your investment strategy that will have an impact on your returns, which in turn will determine your income for the rest of your life. So am I still being dramatic?

8 Running with wolves

The myriad of investment options

I am not going to delve into technical descriptions of different investment types, why a unit trust is better than a Bond or why you would be better investing that spare £10,000 in a Pension rather than an ISA. Bonds, Pensions, ISA, Unit Trusts and OEICs are all vehicles to carry your funds to their destination, containers moulded by man and legislation in which to hold your chosen investments. Which vehicles are most appropriate for your investments to travel in will be decided during discussions with your Adviser. I want to look more deeply at what is held within them and why, to give you a greater understanding of differing investment philosophies and the reasons behind them.

The events of the past decade have thrown the investment world into confusion; accepted ideologies about what worked have been severely challenged and created further uncertainty in an arena where there were not an awful lot of certainties to start with. The so-called experts have repeatedly been proved spectacularly wrong and deeply held beliefs have been put to the test with catastrophe striking across all classes of assets and markets.

Investment statement of intent

Recent uncertainty does not mean that Advisers should shy away from articulating their investment beliefs and documenting them for their clients. This will inevitably mean that at some stage of the economic cycle those beliefs may be found wanting but they should be open to scrutiny and I would be very wary of any Adviser who was unwilling for whatever reason to place those beliefs in writing for you.

A report from the Rotman International Centre for Pension Management found that only 40 of the world's 500 largest Pension funds publish explicit investment beliefs. Previous studies have suggested funds with published investment beliefs achieve better results. This should come as no surprise, whatever endeavour you may be pursuing, if you are documenting what you want to achieve and how you believe it can be achieved will surely give you a head start on those that are unsure what their beliefs are or are unable or unwilling to articulate them.

Part of the problem is that the investment world is fuelled by testosterone, the machismo of work hard, party hard where self belief and taking risks is seen as an act of bravado rather than recklessness, where alpha males pursue alpha returns unhindered by ideology, sometimes at the cost of all else. The focus is on performance not risk, every published investment table highlights returns, no mention is made of the beliefs behind the investment strategy or risk needed to achieve them. There are no prizes for not taking risks, or medals for simply preserving capital. It is those that have made the most, or in recent times lost the least, that win the accolades. Performance is simple to measure and easy to praise or criticise but these simple figures should not be looked at in isolation, they need to be considered in the context of the investment philosophy required to achieve them.

Investment traps to avoid

I am a great believer that you should never invest in something that you don't understand. Investment is a simple subject that has been made hideously complex by so-called experts that are forever developing new ideas to tempt investors. I take a very simple view on every investment proposition that is put to me: 'Would my mum understand this?' Unless the answer is an unequivocal 'yes' I am not interested. The financial disasters that engulfed the world in 2008 demonstrated once again the dangers of entering into things that are unnecessarily complex and difficult, if not impossible, to understand.

We still do not know, despite employing some of the finest minds available, the full extent of the trillions of pounds worth of toxic debt, credit default swaps and other exotic beasts roaming the planet that were designed purely to keep moving the same £1 around the system with everyone taking a penny as it passed them by. There has been a belated realization that economics is not after all a science, but more of an art, sometimes a very black one, that can apply mathematical models to prove virtually anything.

The greater fool theory

From Dutch tulip bulbs to dot com stocks and subprime mortgages, the history of investment is punctuated with stories that prove the greater fool theory will always be with us, despite how sophisticated or informed we believe ourselves to be. As long as there is someone to purchase our investment at a higher price than we paid for it (the greater fool), regardless of its actual worth, bubbles will continue to inflate, until of course we run out of greater fools and the bubble bursts.

So before we really start to consider your investment options, three things to avoid;

1. Fashion

2. Products you don't understand

3. Structured products

Fashion

The investment industry can only really make money by attracting new monies into their funds and so are constantly innovating and reinventing old ideas, dressing them up in trendy buzzword terminology to persuade you the next success story is at your fingertips, and your share of it is only a signature away.

Whole sectors have grown out of these innovations, a newfound success for the investment industry has been Absolute Return Funds, what a great idea, you make money if the market goes up and you make money if the market goes down. 'To deliver a positive return in all stock market conditions' (Octopus Investments). Fantastic! You could be forgiven for thinking that these might be a safe haven for your money in these uncertain times and Absolute Return Funds have proved hugely popular with investors in recent years. Unfortunately it hasn't quite worked out like the marketing hype promised and many investors have been sat nursing losses.

What I find particularly galling about Absolute Return Funds are the performance-related fees Fund Managers award themselves for beating an arbitrary target that they themselves set. Should their funds grow by even a modest amount they will receive a bonus in addition to all the other fees payable by you the client that can be as much as 15% (Jupiter) or 20% (Gartmore) of any returns made on your money. Do they refund you money when they underperform their target? You can guess the answer to that question.

Of the 44 funds in the Absolute Return Sector only 25 have produced a positive return over the last 12 months (Trustnet as at 30.06.10) when world stock markets have been generally rising. Our friends Octopus quoted above have returned -16.9%, nothing really absolute about that. The greatest exponent of these was Blackrock and such was the success of their marketing campaign that the ISA season of 2009 saw them taking more ISA monies than all other funds put together. Staggeringly, investors abandoned their previously considered investment strategies to buy into this new idea that was absolutely going to give them a return. For the record Blackrock Absolute Return returned -0.7% over the last 12 months. Such are the vagaries of fashion.

A more enduring invention of the investment industry are new investment themes, the latest of which has been 'best ideas' where a panel of experts (so-called) are brought together to pick what they believe will be the 30 best performing stocks in the world as a result of the innovation and forward thinking of the Companies concerned. They may be right of course, but what if they are wrong? And shouldn't good fund managers be spotting these opportunities anyway?

Next year it will be something else all dressed up in irrefutable logic, presented with all the excitement of Christmas, and thousands more investors will cash in perfectly good investments so they don't miss out on the next big thing, whether it's Blackrock or Blackpool rock. Some will be successful.

Products you don't understand

None of us wish to appear stupid so when an investment proposition is placed before us that we don't understand so we don't really want to expose our perceived ignorance by pointing out that it makes no sense. The world of investment is full of individuals who earn a living being professional admirers of the Emperor's new clothes and it can be very difficult to ignore the deafening roar of opinion in rising markets – who would not want to be a part of the success and enjoy the financial benefits? Even if you are not sure exactly why and how those benefits arise. It is only when the Emperor's nakedness becomes apparent that you realize the fragility of your investment, by which time it is too late.

Regardless of the Emperor's sartorial state there is an innate belief that the more complex something is the more valuable it must be. There is an element of showboating by Advisers who can showcase their investment knowledge and let their ego out for a stroll by demonstrating their understanding of the complicated world of international investment markets. They can use all the latest buzzwords and talk about hedging and call options and derivatives and you can't help but be impressed. There is also an understandable desire to proudly show you, their client, that they have their finger on the investment pulse and bringing these elaborate investments to your attention shows how hard they are working on your behalf. If you don't understand and no-one can explain it to your satisfaction don't invest in it.

Structured products

It is small-minded to dismiss a whole class of investment products outright but in this instance I will make an exception. There are a seemingly endless stream of nightmare stories involving so-called structured products, many of which are sold by the banks and building societies as secure investments, the Norwich & Peterborough is the latest traditional institution to see its good name tarnished due to the Keydata Bond scandal (Keydata investors are collectively down an estimated £200m).

These investments are usually sold as a capital guaranteed product with benefits, however when you look at the small print your benefits may actually be dependent upon a number of complex factors. This is the kind of thing they spout on about in their glossy brochures, "your capital will be returned in full on the 5th anniversary regardless of stock market conditions and you will benefit from 50% of the growth in the rise in the FTSE100 on the strike date which will be the third Thursday in November" Unless, of course, whoever is underwriting our guarantees goes to the wall, and it happens to be raining on the third Thursday in November or it is dependent upon the FTSE not falling by more than 10% on a day that is between Monday and Friday or whatever complicated conditions may be lurking in the small print. The point I am trying to make is that structured products come with a lot of small print, they are opaque and difficult to analyse.

These were labelled in the press 'precipice Bonds' during a previous scandal and with good reason, many investors had watched their investments fall off a cliff. This leads me to another key concern with these products, it can be very difficult to establish where the responsibility for any guarantees actually resides should things not go according to plan, so I am always keen to find out who is actually holding the parcel should the music stop?

Many of these products appear to eradicate risk, when in fact they are embracing a whole new set of risks, and as you know risk in all its forms is the starting point for every investment decision you will ever make. The consumer magazine *Which?* recently described structured products as "impossibly complicated". Enough said.

Optimising portfolios through asset allocation

So disregarding my three personal cardinal sins of investment outlined above, what are your choices when it comes to investment strategy? Asset allocation theory is repeatedly proving to be the only sound set of investment principals that have been shown to work over the long term. It has been developed around the theories of Professor Harry Markowitz who won the Nobel Prize for his treatise on investment, the award-winning 'Modern Portfolio Theory'.

Modern Portfolio Theory works on the understanding that successful investing is 90% asset allocation and 10% investment choice. Too many people focus solely on investment choice, when it is asset allocation that has repeatedly been shown to be the prime cause of successful long-term investing.

The Markowitz model is a systematic technique for building an investment portfolio and adjusting it over time to ensure it meets the required objectives. It does not attempt to time the markets, so is not affected by short-term fluctuations in investments. The model develops a portfolio, based upon sound asset allocation rules, and then invests to meet the allocation requirements appropriate to your timeframe and attitude to investment risk.

What do we mean by asset allocation?

Before we discuss asset allocation, first of all let us consider what we mean by 'correlation', which in this context is the relationship between two or more investments and the degree to which their values simultaneously change, either positively or negatively.

Individual investments in the same sort of asset tend to be highly correlated. This means they will largely react in the same way to economic and market changes. If one Balanced Managed fund drops, all Balanced Managed funds will drop to a greater or lesser degree. If one Bond Fund drops all Bond Funds will tend to drop. So it does not make sense to invest in a range of Balanced Managed Funds as they will react the same way. This is why we allocate your funds in a mixture of asset classes (different types of investments) in the appropriate percentages – asset allocation. It is particularly important so that your portfolio is holding a range of assets that are not highly correlated; for example; when equities tend to fall, Bonds tend to rise, and vice versa.

We initially incorporate the traditional four asset classes of equities, Bonds, property and cash and as this type of planning grows more sophisticated we can include commodities, hedge funds, indeed anything that is considered an asset class in its own right. Once we have decided upon our global asset allocation, for example we may conclude that 35% of your portfolio should be in equities, we then need to drill down to the next level to decide what proportion should be in the UK, US, Europe, Emerging Markets and so forth.

We know diversifying your portfolio can reduce risk, yet still provide you with the opportunity for investment growth and augment longer-term returns, but that diversity can take many different forms. We are not only considering diversity between asset classes such as equities and Bonds, we are then diversifying equities between the UK and the rest of the world, large Companies and small Companies, growth and value stocks, financials and miners and so asset allocation and in turn diversity can take place on several different levels.

Below are some sample asset allocations for a 'Balanced' investor that have been determined by using the asset allocation tools of some of the leading insurance Companies. Whilst they may be slightly different in their composition the underlying message is the same. An optimal portfolio is simply the mix of assets that maximizes portfolio return at a given risk level by combining different asset classes.

Same theory - different results same outcome

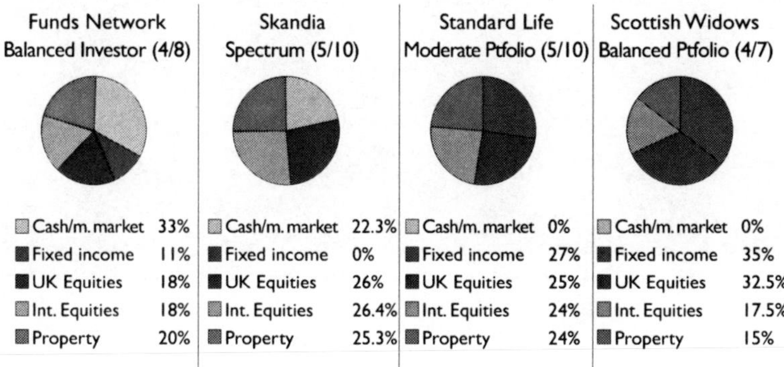

Sources: www.skandia.co.uk www.scottishwidows.co.uk www.fidelity.co.uk www.adviserzone.co.uk

Why do we need to diversify?

Why not simply invest in the best performing sector and regularly move funds around? Nothing wrong with that as long as you know what the best performing sector is going to be over the next 12 months, and looking over your shoulder at what has gone before is of very limited use. With 1,894 funds to choose from in the 'UK All Companies' sector alone, the odds of picking the best fund 3 years in a row are 6,794,224,983 to 1, so a little difficult I am sure you would agree.

It is unusual for the best-performing asset class or stock market in any given year to repeat the trick. Just because it happens to be top of the pops this year is absolutely no guarantee that it will be top of the pops next year. You only have to look at the diagram below to realize the huge variance of returns that can occur between diffierent asset classes. A mixed portfolio, properly asset allocated may be missing out on some of the highs but will also avoid most of the lows and should provide a reasonable return with the diversity within it reducing your overall level of risk.

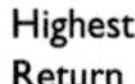

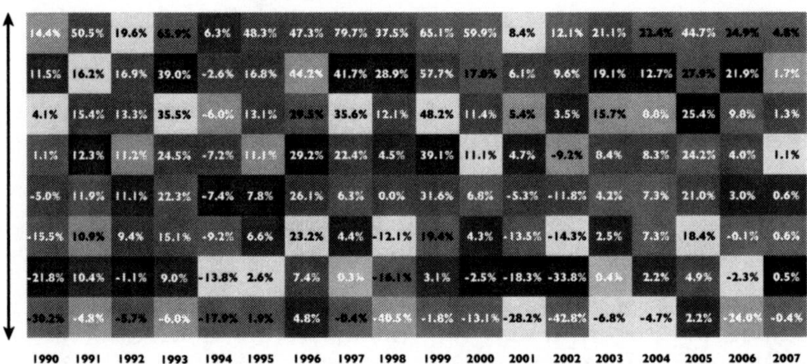

14.4% 50.5% 19.6% 65.9% 6.3% 48.3% 47.3% 79.7% 37.5% 65.1% 59.9% 8.4% 12.1% 21.1% 22.4% 44.7% 34.9% 4.8%
11.5% 16.2% 16.9% 39.0% -2.6% 16.8% 44.2% 41.7% 28.9% 57.7% 17.0% 6.1% 9.6% 19.1% 12.7% 27.9% 21.9% 1.7%
4.1% 15.4% 13.3% 35.5% -6.0% 13.1% 29.5% 35.6% 12.1% 48.2% 11.4% 5.4% 3.5% 15.7% 8.8% 25.4% 9.8% 1.3%
1.1% 12.3% 11.2% 24.5% -7.2% 11.1% 29.2% 22.4% 4.5% 39.1% 11.1% 4.7% -9.2% 8.4% 8.3% 24.2% 4.0% 1.1%
-5.0% 11.9% 11.1% 22.3% -7.4% 7.8% 26.1% 6.3% 0.0% 31.6% 6.8% -5.3% -11.8% 4.2% 7.3% 21.0% 3.0% 0.6%
-15.5% 10.9% 9.4% 15.1% -9.2% 6.6% 23.2% 4.4% -12.1% 19.4% 4.3% -13.5% -14.3% 2.5% 7.3% 18.4% -0.1% 0.6%
-21.8% 10.4% -1.1% 9.0% -13.8% 2.6% 7.4% 0.3% -16.1% 3.1% -2.5% -18.3% -33.8% 0.4% 2.2% 4.9% -2.3% 0.5%
-30.2% -4.8% -5.7% -6.0% -17.9% 1.9% 4.8% -0.4% -40.5% -1.8% -13.1% -28.2% -42.8% -6.8% -4.7% 2.2% -24.0% -0.4%
1990 1991 1992 1993 1994 1995 1996 1997 1998 1999 2000 2001 2002 2003 2004 2005 2006 2007

Lowest
Return

There is no consistent best performing investment. The best this year might be the worst next year

Consistently selecting "the best" performing asset is very hard

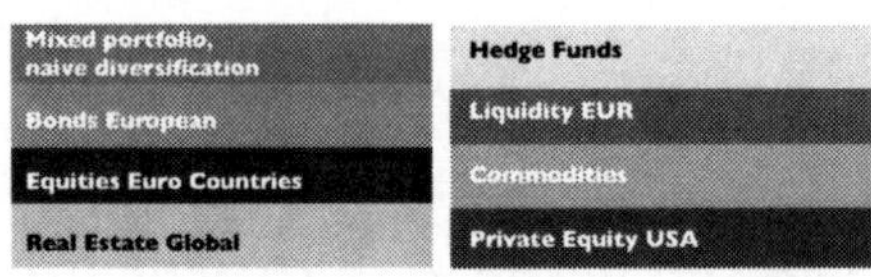

The efficient frontier

Professor Harry Markowitz, the Godfather of asset allocation, demonstrated that for every level of risk it is possible to construct an investment portfolio that delivers a maximum investment return commensurate with that particular level of risk.

This is beacuse for a particular investment portfolio we can illustrate the potential return for the level of risk you are exposed to. In fact, if we constructed several diffierent portfolios that exposed you to the same amount of risk, some would give a better return than others and, inevitably therefore, one would be the best. The portfolio with the mix of assets giving the best return for a particular level of risk is considered the most efficient.

In our simplified example below we have blended six hypothetical portfolios of equities and Bonds over a 100-year period to demonstrate the different levels of return for differing degrees of risk. If we considered ourselves a high risk investor we would probably elect for the portfolio furthest to the right (invested 100% in equities) giving us an annual return of 10.1%. If we were a cautious investor we would probably choose the 100% Bonds portfolio, but this would not necessarily be the most efficient for a cautious investor.

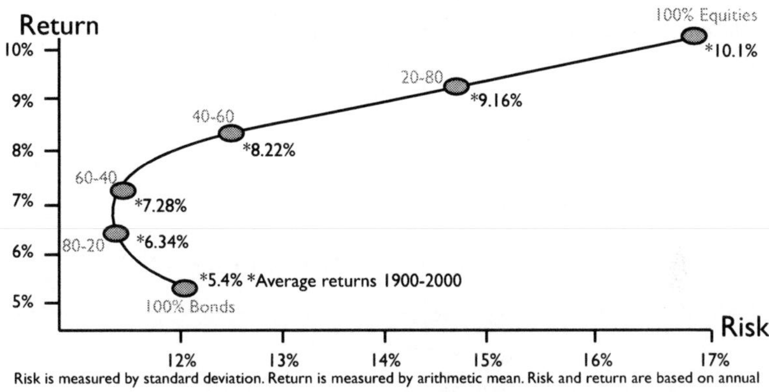

Risk is measured by standard deviation. Return is measured by arithmetic mean. Risk and return are based on annual data over the period 1900-2000. Portfolios presented are based on Modern Portfolio Theory. Source - R.A.M. LLP

However what our graph demonstrates is that it is possible to actually reduce risk and have a more efflcient portfolio by adding higher risk equities into the mix as our portfolios returning 6.34% and 7.28% are actually lower risk (further to the left on our horizontal risk axis) than our 100% Bond portfolio returning a lower 5.4%, so as a cautious investor these would be your most efficient portfolios even though at first glance they may appear higher risk than the

100% Bond portfolio.

Asset allocation – getting the ingredients right

The landmark study, 'Determinants of Portfolio Performance' (*Financial Analysts Journal* 1986) showed that over 90% of investment performance is derived from asset allocation, not market timing or stock selection.

Historically, investment decisions taken by Advisers focused on which particular funds to choose, regardless of what asset class or sector a fund was in. Investment research has repeatedly shown that in the majority of circumstances asset allocation is the critical factor in determining investment performance over the longer term. The Government-sponsored Sandler Report stated in the strongest terms; ***"The asset allocation decision is by far the most important factor in determining returns".***

Apart from the Government's own study let's consider other research in recent years:

Determinants of return

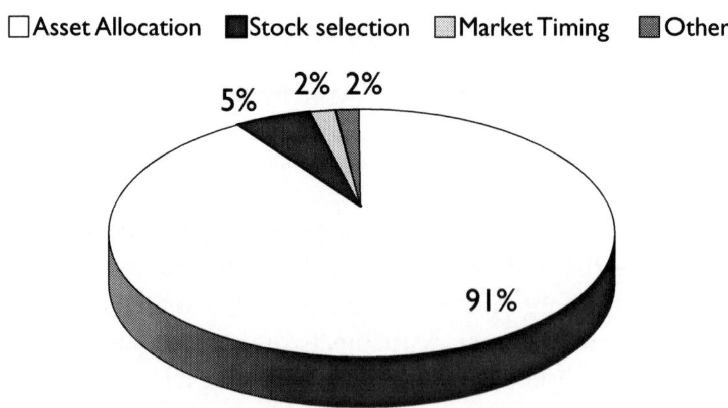

(Source: Brinson Singer Beebower 1991)

Also Ibbotson Associates' report in 2000 showed that 91% of investment returns were derived from asset allocation and research by Fama and French at the University of Chicago once again confirmed our asset allocation beliefs, although more sophisticated, and looking beyond simple asset allocation as a reason for returns their conclusions were the same – more than 90% of investment returns are generated as a result of asset allocation.

As there is substantial evidence from a range of reputable sources we would be foolhardy to ignore many years of research, much of which is common sense, but there are other significant factors that will influence the constituent parts of your portfolio.

How do we arrive at your particular asset allocation?

Asset allocation will vary between investors, but will primarily be decided by three factors:

1. The length of the investment term.

2. Investment goals and objectives.

3. Attitude to risk.

Arriving at an appropriate asset allocation has been made possible by the advent of investment software which assists us by making millions of calculations in less than a second to arrive at an asset allocation model based upon thousands of hypothetical portfolios (Scholastic modelling).

There are numerous variables and assumptions made which means that different software can arrive at different results for the same individual, but one thing research repeatedly demonstrates is that asset allocation should form the cornerstone of your investment strategy.

Rebalancing your portfolio

Once established it is vital to ensure your asset allocation does not become skewed and in doing so becomes inappropriate for your financial objectives in terms of risk/reward. As your investments grow, those in the higher risk area will usually start to outperform the medium and low-risk areas over the longer term. This will have the effiect of putting the portfolio out of balance, as you could have a larger proportion of your investment in higher risk than may be appropriate for your correct asset allocation and attitude to risk. It is vitally important that you reallocate investments regularly to bring your portfolio back into balance. Rebalancing therefore must be an integral part of any investment proposition you wish to consider.

Over time as your investment horizon shortens the asset allocation model ususally reduces your exposure to stock market risk and potential returns are sacrificed in exchange for capital security which usually becomes a greater priority as the years progress. This, of course, varies from individual to individual. After agreeing an appropriate asset allocation that is right for your risk profile and investment timescale, the next question to consider is which type of investment style is best suited to your personal requirement?

9 The tyranny of choice

Your Personal Portfolio

The investment world is always buzzing with debate as to what is the best investment style and as technology drives change at an unprecedented pace, there is seemingly no end to the esoteric permutations that are developed as the next biggest and best way of investing your money. This chapter will take a brief canter through the more well-known styles and ones that you are likely to encounter in conversation with Advisers as well as draw your attention to some other factors that could affiect your returns long term.

Without doubt one of the major contests in recent years has been between the advocates of passive investing opposing their active management counterparts and as you will almost certainly encounter this debate at some point on your investment journey it is worth gaining an understanding of the fundamentals.

What is active and passive investment management?

The clue is in the name, and for ease let's consider two UK Equity funds, one active, one passive, and look at the diffierent way they operate, their costs, and of course the resulting performance. When selecting shares for his fund the active manager will seek to outperform an index or benchmark, while a passive manager will seek to replicate an index such as the FTSE 100. It should be noted that the majority of active managers do not outperform their benchmark and they usually cost more.

Active managers are using research and analysis to help them decide what shares they want to hold within their portfolios, this can involve analysing Company accounts, meeting Company executives, as well as looking at the broader market within that sector and the prospects for it in the near future. The fund manager will use his stock selection skill to try to outperform his competitors. This might be based on superior market knowledge, better research, contacts or simply more sophisticated financial modelling techniques.

Your active fund manager will have a documented remit in respect of what his fund can and cannot invest in, what his philosophy is, and not insignificantly what he is expecting to achieve, with carefully articulated benchmarks to measure the fund manager's performance. These benchmarks will usually be aligned to the average performance within that particular sector and provide focus for the fund manager if for no other reason than his bonus payments will be more than likely linked to them! His bonus may be maximized if he outperforms the sector average by 5%, it may be reduced if he outperforms by 10%. Why? Because the fund trustees do not want him taking reckless risks in pursuit or bonus payments.

There are two additional components of the investment strategy of active investment managers. First, the driving force of emotion, for as much as we all like to dress our decisions in cool analytical logic the emotions play a huge part in any investment decision. One of the strongest emotions in the investment world is fear, very often a fear of missing out or being singled out for being wrong which leads us to the second overlooked component; the herd instinct..

It is no accident that 99% of the UK fund management industry is based in the Square Mile, in these days of technology fund management could be just as effiectively undertaken in the Outer Hebrides. So why do fund managers all want to congregate in one small corner of one of the most expensive and overcrowded cities on God's green earth? Simple; safety in numbers.

This also applies to investment decisions, if one of the bigger managers starts to buy into a particular sector or stock others tend to follow. There are two very simple ways to prove this, just look at the top ten holdings of any particular fund and many of the same names will appear again and again in other funds within the same sector. If you can't be bothered to do that simply look at the graph below which shows five of the leading UK Balanced Managed funds over the past 12 months, do you detect a particular pattern here? Essentially they are indistinguishable with all five investment vehicles pretty much sticking to the same matching roller coaster track.

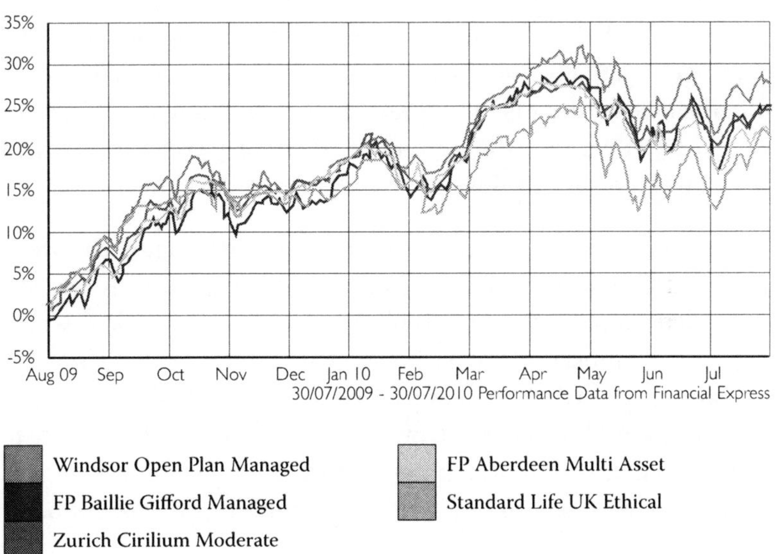

Relax and be passive

By comparison passive funds are not actively buying and selling shares based on research, emotion or anything else. They are simply seeking to replicate an index such as the FTSE 100 or the Eurostoxx 50 so that your returns will reflect the movement in the underlying index. Your fund will be a mirror of the index it is trying to track so that if the FTSE 100 rises 11% over the year so does your passive FTSE 100 tracker fund. If the FTSE 100 falls 6% over the year so does your fund.

Passive funds seek to hold exactly the same components as their chosen index so in our FTSE 100 example if the three largest FTSE 100 Companies (for example) are HSBC, which by value constitutes 6% of the index, Shell which constitutes 4% of the index and Vodafone 3%. A FTSE 100 tracker fund seeks to hold those funds within the same proportion within it. If by next week, HSBC has dropped to 5.9% of the FTSE 100 by value, the holding within your fund will also have dropped to 5.9%.

Passive funds can come in a multitude of structures from simple Trackers which fully replicate the index they are tracking to Exchange Traded Funds which use synthetic sampling (meaning they are not actually holding any funds at all, just a complex series of financial instruments to simulate their chosen index). This is not the place to dive into the myriad of different passive investment styles, but I am sure by now you have grasped the concept.

Passive fund management makes no attempt to distinguish between 'good' and 'bad' Companies, predict market movements or forecast future share prices, it simply replicates the chosen market, which is usually composed of the strongest Companies in the economy. Exposure to international equity markets through Tracker funds reduces risk and an element of overseas exposure allows you to participate in any potential growth of the global economy, as well as providing diversity to reduce volatility within your portfolio.

Passives offer several advantages over actively managed funds, for a start they don't really require any managing at all, most of the trading is automated and no teams of researchers or analysts are required, nor are any bonus-devouring fund managers. The computer busily trading stocks for you can work 24 hours a day without a lunch break, will not develop a cocaine problem nor be caught in a compromising grapple with Eastern European lap dancers. Most importantly none of its investment decisions will be influenced by human emotion, it will simply stick to the mandate it was programmed with, and it will not be swayed by opinion or fashion, or any deep emotional need to follow the herd.

It is also the simplicity and transparency that makes Passives appealing, they can provide massive diversity and you know what you are going to get in terms of returns by looking at the index they are tracking.

Passive funds are also very cheap to run and Annual Management Charges of less than 0.5% are now common, compared to Actively Managed funds which can comfortably charge you 1.5% per annum. It may not seem like an awful lot but look at the effects of charging and ask yourself, would you pay three times as much for a car that will still only get you from A to B? All the evidence suggests that for the vast majority of people the answer to that question bizarrely is yes!

IF YOU'RE TORN BETWEEN ACTIVE AND PASSIVE MANAGEMENT OUR PASSIVE ACTIVE MANAGER MAY SUIT

There is no evidence that active fund management is successful

The active fund management industry spends huge sums of money persuading the public they have the next success story, but even if a fund has a track record to date, what guarantee is there it will deliver in the future? There is minimal scientific evidence that in general terms active fund management is more successful than the passive approach. In fact there is little evidence to suggest that active fund managers can consistently produce returns any better than a blindfolded chimpanzee throwing darts. If there was such evidence fund managers would be shouting it from the rooftops.

The active managers' claim is that they add value to your portfolio in the form of improved returns, beating the index or whatever sector average they happen to be in, but are they right? They certainly cost more and to justify their overpaid existence and that of their team we need to see this performance made flesh. It is often quoted that 80% of active managers fail to outperform the index they are trying to beat, so if you have an 80% chance of ending up with a return less than you could realistically expect from a passive tracker fund run for a third of the price, why bother?

Could it be because over 10 years to 30.06.10 the top 10 active funds in the IMA UK All Companies sector returned 111.9% on average compared with just 16.9% from the 15 FTSE All Share Tracker funds with a 10 year track record.

It's emotion again, we are all hoping to be in that top 10 of star performers, sharing in the benefits of premier league fund management. Logically of course we cannot all be in that glorious top 10 but, as you know, logic only plays a small part in investing, emotionally we believe we can be, and are still prepared to try even though the evidence of making it is firmly against us.

As always there is no right or wrong answer and many Advisers are opting for a combination of both approaches, applying passives to the strategic asset allocation and then selecting a number of specialist funds to provide some tactical overlay to take advantage of current market opportunities.

Certainly there is a a lack of independent evidence to support the active approach to fund management but that does not mean that there are not Advisers and investment houses that are still beating their chosen Index on a regular basis, because if they were not why would their clients stay with them? It is estimated that only 3% of funds purchased in 2009 were Tracker funds, so even assuming this is a gross underestimate, the vast majority of Advisers and investors are still buying actively managed funds, so would investors and their clients continue to pay higher charges for continued underperformance? It would seem unlikely.

Core & satellite portfolio management

Is an investment strategy that integrates traditional Fixed Income & Equity passive funds (such as Trackers and Exchange Traded Funds) for the majority 'core' portion of the portfolio, with a percentage of specially selected individual actively managed funds around the edge of the portfolio known as the 'satellite' element.

Generally the passives are held for the long term with the satellite funds being more actively bought and sold by your Adviser. The idea is that the core holdings will provide diversity and steady growth with the active funds providing that turbo charged boost to performance to lift your portfolio above the average whilst keeping management costs reasonable. The best of both worlds? That will depend entirely upon your individual portfolio and the skill of the Adviser actively selecting your funds, especially the satellite element, which will be the key determinant of your returns.

Guaranteed Funds

In the same way that you would insure your car or your house, you can now pay an insurance premium to protect your Pension or investment fund against loss, this potentially makes the active versus passive decision redundant as you can now select from a number of managed portfolios that will never fall in value. Too good to be true? Well maybe, it depends upon what your priorities are.

These funds work by locking in any growth on each anniversary of the investment; this also locks in a boost to any income you may be receiving. If there has been no growth in the underlying fund, or indeed there has been a fall in value, your fund remains unchanged; essentially it can only go up.

Before you get carried away by this investment utopia in a perfect world where bad things can't happen to investors, be warned that your insurance premium to protect against loss could be as much as 1.5% every year. Also you will have an above average annual management charge on your fund with very little room for manoeuvre as to where you can invest so there is limited control over the underlying investments. It could well be that you don't care as you can look at the financial news without anxiety and laugh mockingly at stock market crashes with the smug satisfaction that your Pension pounds will be largely unaffected.

Apart from cost there are two other significant downsides to consider, there is usually a maximum return you can achieve each year that can be locked in, normally 10%. Secondly if you move away from the Company providing the guarantee then the guarantee is lost so you will have paid for nothing and you will receive the underlying value of the assets which could be a lot less than the guaranteed value.

While such a strategy may limit your returns in the longer term, protection against loss can be a valuable asset, as can the certainty of a guaranteed income in the future. As always this route is a compromise and like so many of the options in this book is not exclusive, it can be used in tandem with other options to achieve your longer-term goals, and if capital security or a guaranteed and rising income were on your wish list, it could play a valuable part.

Real life...

Dave retired at the start of 2009 and wanted to guarantee a portion of his income for life to cover all his living expenses. We therefore agreed to place 50% of his Pension fund in a guaranteed fund giving him a guaranteed income for life. The other 50% was placed in a stock market fund in an Income Drawdown plan which paid a higher income, 7% compared to 4% in his guaranteed fund.

2009 saw markets rise and Dave's income Drawdown fund went up 22%. Because of the restrictions placed upon his guaranteed fund (and attaching income) it could only go up 10% so Dave was a touch disappointed. Only time will tell if that disappointment increases or turns to relief if markets plummet.

Different approach for different assets

You may want to take a different view for different assets; you might decide to speculate more with your ISA, while playing cautious with your Pension fund or you may decide a proportion of your Pension needs to be rock solid secure, whatever that means these days. You will still arrive at an attitude to risk which brings us back to asset allocation. You should consider all of your assets in the round, if you consider an asset allocation model and it recommends 20% of your assets to be in cash, that doesn't mean you have to place 20% of your Pension assets in cash if you already have 20% of your total assets sat sitting in cash in the bank.

Britain's most popular fund - make sure you're not in it

Every week of my life I meet people who have their Pension invested in Britain's most popular fund, some have been in it for 20 years or more and my first job is usually to move them out of it because as soon as they discover why it's so popular they strangely decide it's not for them. What fund am I referring to?

The Apathy Fund. By far Britain's most popular, and it is also the most lucrative but only for the fund managers concerned. I am always amazed that someone who would normally consider themselves prudent is quite happy to leave their Pension fund invested with a Company where they don't know what they're getting charged for having it managed and absolutely no idea what level of returns they have been receiving. I regularly meet people who don't even know what fund they are invested in and it's not unusual for people to not even know what insurance Company their Pension is invested with ("err... it's Scottish something").

It's a familiar tale, someone sells you a Pension, or you join a scheme with your employer and you never see the person who set it up again or the person you're dealing with is different every year and they're not interested in reviewing your funds because there is no commission in that for them so they brush over that issue and look to sell you something else.

The whole insurance industry is structured to avoid reviewing funds and this works in their favour, avoiding any uncomfortable conversations about poor performance or outdated charges that are expensive by modern standards. As a customer where do you turn for a review? How do you even know if you need one? Funds should be reviewed once a year, when was the last time you reviewed yours? Companies rely on your apathy to boost their profit margins. Staying in the Apathy fund could cost you thousands of pounds and have a serious impact on your retirement income. It's Britain's most popular fund but only with the fund providers.

Real life...

Brian runs a builders merchants in South Shields and it is no joke that copper wire was invented as a result of him and his wife arguing over a penny. If he can haggle 0.01p off the price of a ton of bricks from his supplier he surely will. Concerned about his Pension fund which "has been going nowhere fast for years" he wanted me to undertake a fund review. When I told him our fee for this service, he went pale and started to swoon, saying he had to think about it. After 2 years of thinking about it he came back, still anxious about the fee, sucking wind through his teeth in that anxious way that everyone in the building trade seems to have down to a fine art whenever the subject of money is raised. Reluctantly he gave me the go ahead on the basis that the financial pain of doing something was actually less than the financial pain of doing nothing.

On the advice of his Accountant in a bid to cut his tax liability Brian had made a single Pension contribution of £50,000 in the late 1980s into a Personal Pension with Abbey Life. On the advice of the salesman Brian's money was invested in the Abbey Life Managed fund. So after almost 20 years in the Managed (or should that be Apathy?) fund how had he fared? The fund had ticked along providing average returns so how come Brian's £50,000 was now only worth £48,687?

Without going into the vagaries of the charging structure applied to Brian's Abbey Life Pension plan it was charges that had caused the damage as much as the mediocre performance. What had Brian's unconscious enthusiasm for the Apathy fund really cost him? It is impossible to calculate, the paper loss of £1,313 is easy to see, but what about the damage 20 years of inflation had done to the value of his £50k, what about all he had paid in charges, what about all of the investment performance forgone if he had paid for advice? Even a modest 4% a year net of charges would have turned Brian's £50,000 into a far more respectable £105,000.

Brian is a very ordinary example of Britain's most popular fund but there are millions more Brians out there. Make sure you are not one of them.

The effect of charges on your investments

There are substantial amounts of newsprint dedicated to the 'wasteful' and 'scandalous' charges applied to investment products and the detrimental effects they have on investors' returns. They do of course have an effect on your ultimate return, but they need to be considered in perspective. The reason journalists focus on them is because it's easy, any lazy financial journalist short of copy can soon knock up a piece about the charges being levied on funds. As always it is not just about cost it is about the value those costs bring to your portfolio.

Charges are a factor for consideration, an element in the mix; they are not the deciding factor for me as to whether I should invest in a particular fund. A high annual management charge would not preclude me from investing and at the same time the lowest charge on the market would not be enough to secure my patronage. It is the other factors that will have greater emphasis on that decision such as performance, the prospects for the fund in the future and so on.

Once again there is no evidence that low charging funds provide better performance than their high charging counterparts or that higher charging funds are more wasteful or badly managed.

In the same way low charges are not enough in isolation we do want to ensure we avoid the worst of all worlds - high charges and poor performance. Investment charges are undoubtedly on a downward trend, partly due to market pressures but mostly due to the relentless advance of technology.

It is important to remember when looking at cost to compare like with like. For example, the HSBC UK Tracker Cash Fund can be bought by a retail investor like yourself for an annual charge of 0.15%; the Invesco Perpetual Emerging Countries Fund will cost you 1.5 % per year, so why would you want to pay ten times as much?

The two funds are completely different, the Tracker fund as I am sure you can guess by now is a fully automated deposit fund, the Invesco Perpetual is far more complex, investing in markets which are difficult to research and expensive to deal in, but where returns (and risk!) are way in excess of what the HSBC Cash Fund could produce. Fundamentally they fulfil the same function but so do a Ferrari and a Ford Focus.

TER, PTR and other charges to create confusion

The Annual Management Charge for the day-to-day management of your holding by the fund manager is easy to identify and calculate which is why so many journalists latch on to it, but it only tells part of the story. Below the waterline there are other charges in the murky depths of fund management that are not necessarily visible to the naked eye.

Every regulated fund must publish a Total Expenses Ratio (TER), but the interesting thing about a Total Expense Ratio is that it does not include the total of all expenses nor is it a ratio! It does include the annual management charge plus other running costs such as trustee fees, audit fees and the FSA fee so it does provide a more honest indication of the charges being levied on your pounds. However, it does not include preliminary or dealing costs. As part of the dealing cost you have to pay Stamp Duty of 0.5% every time a share is purchased so this can potentially be substantial.

One of the costs of running a fund is the actual dealing of the underlying investments within it. Every time an asset is bought or sold a cost is incurred so the more times during the year assets are bought and sold the more costs will be incurred. The PTR (Portfolio Turnover Rate) provides a measurement of how often assets within your selected fund are bought and sold. In simple turns a PTR of 100% means that during a 12-month period, every asset within your portfolio has been sold and replaced, a PTR of 50% means that half of the assets within your fund have been sold within the last 12 months. Even the modest costs of trading within a tracker fund plus stamp duty on every deal will have a drag on your returns. Again it's not significant by itself, but is another factor in the mix and one to consider.

Real life…

I invested in the Close UK Special Situations Fund, just a modest punt as I felt it could do well as the UK came out of recession in 2009. For a while it produced some excellent returns. I read in the fund prospectus that it had a PTR of 247%, with a TER of 1.86% so a very actively managed fund and all that activity incurs cost. When returns are top drawer do I care? Not one jot! Go for it Mr Fund manager, buy and sell your soul for all I care.

How about when my funds are going down and I'm no longer in that top drawer? Mmm... maybe I care a bit more now about all those costs.

Adviser fund charge

In addition there will be your Adviser's fee for monitoring your funds, which can be more than the annual management charge on the funds themselves, and in my biased and totally subjective view, so they should be as the Adviser is the key to carefully choosing funds and managing your investment strategy to produce the returns you are expecting.

No-one is going to lay on their death bed being grateful for having invested in funds with the lowest charges, but they may be grateful they achieved the returns that allowed them to live out their retirement the way they chose too.

"Congratulations Mr Client, after 10 years of investing your returns have been poor but you have had the lowest charges in the market place." Not a sentence anyone would welcome I'm sure.

I realize there is some technical jargon in this chapter, and it's not over yet, but I wanted to provide you with an opportunity to look under the bonnet of the various investment styles available to you so that when your Adviser starts talking active/passive or core/satellite you are ahead of the game and will not only have some advanced understanding of what is on offer but may also have some idea of the investment philosophy you will be most comfortable with over the coming years. There is no best way, no one golden panacea, otherwise we would all be doing it and there would no decisions to make.

As always with investment styles there is no right or wrong answer, different styles will work better at different times in the economic cycle, in different sectors or different markets. The only thing that we can be reasonably certain about is that an asset allocation appropriate to your appetite for risk has the potential to generate returns while providing you with enough diversity to protect against the worst outcome.

There will be an optimum solution to provide you with the most suitable investment strategy to suit your circumstances today and it is one that should be adaptable enough to accommodate your changing requirements as the years advance. Whatever your investment strategy there are two sharks forever lurking beneath the surface, they are always swimming, they never stop, constantly hunting out new sources of food, and if you are not vigilant or simply ill-advised they will take ever bigger bites out of your retirement income, we will look at these two merciless beasts in the next chapter.

10 Beware the two-headed Hydra

Defeating inflation and tax

Are there two more dull subjects? A whole chapter dedicated to such tedium? Yes! Because they are vitally important and it will only be a short chapter I promise.

Getting a grip on inflation

First of all let's get a grip on what exactly inflation means for you. In the UK we use two main measures; the Retail Price Index and the Consumer Prices Index and both purchase a hypothetical basket of thousands of goods every month based upon the typical spend of some mythical average UK household.

There are differences between the shopping baskets of the two measures, notably CPI does not include housing costs or Council Tax which can be a significant proportion of peoples' living expenses. The prices of these baskets of goods are then compared with the prices of those self same goods 12 months ago and an average assumed to ascertain any change. The calculation of the two measures is undertaken slightly differently (using a geometric rather than arithmetic mean if you care!) which results in CPI rising at a lower rate than RPI. Such calculations may not seem significant but the Institute of Fiscal Studies estimates that a switch from RPI to CPI in respect of index linking state benefits amounts to a 5% reduction in real terms over a 5-year period.

State Pensions, as discussed in Chapter 3, are going to be revalued every year on the 'triple lock' basis which is to be welcomed but the majority of Company Pensions currently work off the RPI figure when calculating your annual increase. Historically the month when inflation is frequently at its lowest is September, care to hazard a guess which month the Government use to base their figure for next year's index linking rise? Of course! The rate of inflation in September is the rate applied the following April for the next 12 months.

No such 'triple lock' protection is offered for private sector Pension schemes that are going to be permitted to increase benefits in line with CPI also, saving them an estimated £100bn, which means that's £100bn less paid out in Pensions to members like you. Much was made of Gordon Brown's £5bn tax raid on Pensions, I have even been known to comment upon it myself occasionally, but that was nothing in comparison. It is estimated that 12 million Pensioners will be £8,300 worse off over the course of their retirement. To put this change into perspective, if you started drawing your Pension 22 years ago when CPI was first calculated and your increases had been based upon it, your Pension today would be worth 16% less than if your increase had been linked to RPI, quite a difference. So it's great news for shareholders and Directors, yet more grim news for members of Pension schemes.

The silent assassin of your lifestyle

Inflation is a highly personal thing, the news might claim inflation over the last 12 months has only been 1.2% but it certainly doesn't feel like that in my house, it feels more like 12%. Now inflation may indeed be 1.2% if you have purchased that mythical basket of goods, but as I don't go out every month and buy a BluRay disc player, allergy tablets and hair straighteners, it's of very limited relevance as a figure for planning my finances. If you would like to find out what your very own rate of inflation is visit www.statistics.gov.uk/pic/ and look up the 'Personal Inflation Calculator'. I haven't tried it myself but you can have a play around and see what various different spending patterns make to your very own personal inflation rate.

Inflation is age related

What we spend our money on is largely dependent upon age, not only in terms of our tastes and priorities but simply in terms of our changing lifestyle. As we go through retirement an increasing proportion of our income is spent on fixed costs, most notably utilities and council tax both of which have been increasing at levels way in excess of inflation throughout the last decade. These costs are almost impossible to mitigate, yes you can turn the gas down but do you really want to spend your time wrapped in a quilt in front of the television?

For those of us that were around in the 70s and 80s we have grown rather complacent about inflation because our economy no longer resembles that of Argentina, we no longer regard it as a threat to our lifestyle but low number inflation is still pernicious. A quick glance at the table below shows the kind of damage that even modest inflation can make to your income. Over the last 20 years (1989-2009) prices have risen 83%, (www.thisismoney.co.uk), if we see the same over the next 20 years what will that do to your retirement income?

The effect of inflation on the value of £1,000

Annual Inflation rate	5 Years	10 Years	15 Years	25 years
2.25%	£894	£800	£716	£573
4%	£821	£675	£555	£375
6%	£747	£558	£417	£233
8%	£680	£463	£315	£146

What about savings and investments?

Very few accounts available from the banks or building societies can offer protection against inflation or any real capital growth for the longer term, they are simply the safe option, and it is a case of locating the least bad rate to stem the haemorrhage of your money's value. Best buy table such as those from www.moneyfacts.co.uk will provide you with an insight as to what is currently available. Once you have found the best rate for your needs, deduct the current rate of inflation and tax to work out how much you are left with.

National Savings do provide a genuine safeguard against inflation with index-linked certificates as you are guaranteed a return currently of 1% plus inflation at the end of 5 years, regardless of how high it should be. Clearly not a solution for the spontaneous short-term investor, but a hedge nonetheless. NS&I additionally have the security that your money is absolutely safe, no small advantage in these uncertain times.

The stock market has traditionally provided returns in excess of inflation, but we are back to our old friend risk. Guaranteed Income Bonds from insurance Companies may provide a solution but they require careful examination before investing. There are longer-term investment funds available from insurance Companies that will guarantee you a return of 3-4% per annum for a definite period, with the opportunity for index linking, for life in some cases, but again they require careful scrutiny.

Should you index link your Pension if you are buying an Annuity? Well that's for the next chapter but it needs to be considered in the context of your whole income position, what proportion of your income-producing assets does your Pension Annuity constitute? How critical is that to your longer-term financial well being? If your income does decline will you need to begin eroding your capital to fund your living expenses? What rate of inflation would it take to jeopardize your longer-term income? We need to consider the effect of inflation in the context of your whole investment strategy.

Real life...

Pete and Theresa invest £200,000 and they need an income from it of £18,000 a year so even with a return of 7% their fund will be exhausted in 20.5 years. They are not overly concerned by this as they want to enjoy themselves while they are fit and well. Things are going to be tight so they need to protect their income against inflation and arrange for their income to increase by 2.5% per year. This will mean their fund will be exhausted in just over 15 years. That modest 2.5% increase will shorten the life of their income-producing asset by 25%.

The three certainties in life?

Ben Franklin said there are only two certainties in life – death and taxes – but if you live in the UK there is a third one: being taxed to death! Things have changed slightly, death can now be postponed and will continue to be so but as for taxes, there are more of them than Ben Franklin could ever have dreamed of and unlike inflation which is not a certainty, tax will always be with us in its many mutating and multiplying forms.

Income tax

We are all entitled to a personal allowance, which is the amount we can earn before we are obliged to join the income tax club. In the current tax year of 2010/11 it is £6,475, which increases to £9,490 at age 65. Every penny you receive in income up to this amount has no liability to tax; thereafter you are a paying member of the income tax club

Basic State Pension and income tax

One point which I feel requires repeating as it tends to cause some confusion is the tax position of the Basic State Pension as people tell me it's 'tax free' or 'not liable to income tax' The State Pension is not taxed at source but that does not mean it is not liable to income tax.

For example, you are 65 years old and therefore have a personal allowance of £9,490 (2010/11). Assuming you have no other income in the current tax year other than your Basic State Pension of £5,077.80 you will have no income tax liability. If your income is higher than £9,490 due to the addition of other sources of income you will be liable for income tax on the amount that exceeds the personal allowance. So remember, whilst the State Pension may not be taxed it is indeed taxable and when you add on any other income you may have such as Personal Pensions or Building Society interest you may very well be carried kicking and screaming into the income tax club.

Tax on your Pensions

Usually you will be taxed at source just the same way as the employed pay income tax on earnings via the PAYE system so there's not a lot you can do to mitigate the tax to be paid. You will receive a tax coding notice from HMRC and a P60 every year, it's just like being back at work really! There is always the possibility that you can structure your income to keep your tax burden to a minimum by not commencing income until you have dropped into a lower tax band such as 40% down to 20% or 20% down to a non-taxpayer. However, this could mean delaying taking some or all of your income until after the arrival of another tax year if possible.

Pension commencement lump sum

Prior to the legislative changes in April 2006 this was known simply as 'tax free cash' so are HMRC quietly seeking to change this most favoured of Pension tax breaks? More than likely, but as things stand – providing your scheme rules permit – you can take 25% of your total Pension fund as a tax-free lump sum anytime after your 55th birthday. You don't have to retire and you don't even have to take any income from your Pension, so apart from the obvious attractions of suddenly having a nice tax-free lump sum to do with what you choose what are the implications tax-wise?

First let's state the obvious; if you take 25% of your Pension fund as a cash sum your residual Pension is going to be 25% less for the rest of your life and you are also going to miss out on any investment growth that 25% could have enjoyed. If you are in receipt of Pension benefits that will increase in retirement you are also going to miss out on any increases that 25% would have received if you had taken it as Pension.

Real life...

Geoff is 65-years old, in good health and retiring today with a Pension pot of £100,000. He wants to take his maximum tax-free cash of £25,000 to pay off a small mortgage and book a well-deserved holiday. The best level Annuity rate he can obtain is 6.5% which will give him an income from his £75,000 residual fund guaranteed for life of £4,875 per year (subject to income tax naturally!). He has forgone the income of £1,625 (subject to tax!) in favour of £25,000 tax free cash. Was that a good idea?

As a 20% taxpayer Geoff would need to live for 20 years for it to have been worthwhile to forgo the flexibility and enjoyment of his tax-free lump sum, rather than income which would have been eroded by inflation.

Like all Annuity purchase decisions it's a gamble that you can only bet on once, although in this instance, like Geoff, I would be inclined to take the money and if at age 86 I am proved to be wrong, I don't imagine it will be one of my life's greatest regrets. That, of course, assumes that Geoff spends all his lump sum rather than invest it, and then use it to provide him with a tax-free income for life, potentially the best of both worlds, and a perfectly feasible option.

Even if Geoff were a non-taxpayer (when there is clearly no tax advantage in taking the 25% up front) there is still the benefit of doing what you wish with a lump sum which would take you more than 15 years to recover in the form of tax-free Pension income.

A third way - slice it up!

Instead of making that all-or-nothing tax free cash decision at outset you can consume it in a series of slices that can be different sizes depending upon your tax-free cash appetite. For example, Geoff above wants to draw just 10% of his fund at the start. He therefore withdraws £10,000 and leaves the remainder invested – no problem. A few months later he decides he wants another £5,000 and then next year another £3,600 and so on until he has drawn down his full 25% tax free. Although you need to be aware that once you take £1 as a 'Pension commencement lump sum' HMRC arrive with the barbed wire and searchlights to surround your 25% so that it can never increase in value. Staying with our friend Geoff with his £100,000 fund, if he takes £1 today as tax-free cash and his residual fund grows to £1m he will only ever be able to withdraw a further £24,999 as tax-free cash in the future, the total amount of tax-free cash being ring fenced at £25,000 the first day he makes a withdrawal.

As another alternative, instead of taking all of your tax-free cash on day one, every time you wish to withdraw some income 25% of it can be paid to you tax free. In our example you chop your Pension fund into 100 slices of £1,000 with every slice providing you with £250 tax free and the balance of £750 being used to provide a taxable income.

Lump sums from Company schemes

When exchanging Pension for tax-free cash within a Company Scheme (an exercise strangely known as commuting) the decision requires a little deeper thought because your scheme administrators will have arrived at the commutation factor used to exchange Pension income for tax-free cash. The commutation factor is the cost to you of Pension forgone in exchange for cash and is usually expressed as a ratio.

A commutation factor of 12:1 means that every £12 of tax-free cash you receive you forego £1 a year of Pension income, a commutation factor of 20:1 is a better deal as you get £20 of tax-free cash for every £1 of Pension given up. As every scheme sets its commutation factor independently you need to look below the surface before reaching your decision. As a benchmark for comparison, at current Annuity rates within a Personal Pension the commutation rate is roughly 15:1, so a number larger than this gives you a better rate than you could realistically achieve in the open market. A figure less than 15 suggests the purely financial advantage of taking tax-free cash lies with the scheme rather than you.

Tax on investments can be avoided

Tax is understandably a huge frustration for the retired, you've worked all your life paying tax and still HMRC want their pound of flesh now that you've stopped working, and as you will see later they still want their pound of flesh even after you've stopped living!

The average Pensioner household pays 30% of its income in tax in various forms, with Council Tax a large part of that burden accounting for nearly 5% of gross household income. Whereas Council Tax is a more of a localized issue and you can apply for a reduction depending upon your circumstances, income tax can be mitigated to such a degree as that I have stated previously, it is in large part a voluntary tax and we will look later in this chapter at Capital Gains Tax and the use of Bonds to enjoy more of your income tax-free.

Pensions are an extremely tax-efficient method of investing with the benefit of tax relief on contributions and virtually tax free growth, not to mention their ubiquitous familiarity make them an obvious first stop on your retirement planning journey, but what other investment opportunities are available that offer tax advantages?

Individual Savings Accounts (ISAs)

ISAs have to be the travelling companion of choice for any Pension planning. Most of the tax advantages have been eroded over the years, but two key ones remain; the opportunity to take all of the proceeds of your ISA at anytime in full without any liability to tax and the benefit of having up to £5,100 in a bank or building society account with the interest rolling up gross. With the potential to invest a maximum of £10,200 each and every tax year this has to be the starting point for any additional monies that you hold, even if you have any rainy day funds on deposit, there is no disadvantage in holding them in an ISA, although interest rates are low and therefore the tax savings minimal, better in your pocket than theirs.

Other tax-free opportunities

National Savings & Investments we have already considered and are ideal for a cautious low-risk/return investment. If you want something that is more of a genuine investment opportunity with tax benefits you could contemplate Venture Capital Trusts (maximum investment £200,000 per year) or Enterprise Investment Schemes (maximum investment £300,000 per year).

That makes for tax-free investment of more than half a million pounds a year, more than enough for most people I would suggest. Naturally many of these tax incentives are granted to encourage investors into higher-risk areas of the economy where there is a very real possibility of capital loss but many of these investments can be managed in such a way as to reduce your exposure to risk.

Tax incentives alone should never be reason enough to invest in anything, my point is that there are a range of investment opportunities out there to reduce your tax bill, quite possibly even down to zero and beyond if you really put your mind to it. There are a wide range of options to suit all pockets and risk profiles that permit you to invest with the taxman's blessing so I can only assume a lot of investment income tax is paid by choice, as a kindness by Pensioners who, after working all of their lives, feel a duty to keep contributing to the exchequer. Thank you, but you really don't have to.

Unit trusts/OEICs

If you invest in a stocks and shares ISA, more than likely your funds will be held within a unit trust or Open-ended Investment Company (OEIC). Along with other investors you buy units in a fund which are priced daily based upon the value of the underlying investments. Each day if you wish you can look up the unit price of your chosen fund and you can easily calculate the value of your holding and, if you wish to, buy more units or sell your existing holding – this is a simple and relatively cheap exercise. So what are the tax benefits?

Beyond your ISA allowance there is no limit on the amount of units you can buy. The beauty is that when you sell some or all of your units, either to provide you with an income or to generate a lump sum, the profit you have made is liable to Capital Gains Tax NOT Income Tax. So what? I hear you cry. The point is every individual has an annual Capital Gains Tax allowance of £10,100 (2010/11) so that you may realize profit by selling units and crystallizing a capital gain of up to £10,100 without any liability to tax, if you are a couple this generates additional income up to £20,200 every year tax free.

There are thousands of different OEICs available ranging from the ultra-cautious deposit fund right along the risk spectrum to Brazilian Gas shares so you will easily find several that sit comfortably with your risk profile and income needs. You can be as adventurous or not as you wish.

And more tax benefits...

In addition there are a further two tax advantages of investing in OEICS and using your CGT allowance.

Every year you can move another £10,100 of your OEICs investments under your ISA umbrella so that you have no tax liability whatsoever, freeing up more of your funds to soak up yet more of your annual £10,100 CGT allowance.

If you don't need to sell any units to provide you with an income you can still capitalize on growth within your OEICS by switching between funds and crystallizing the gain. For example, you invest £100,000 and in 12 months' time your £100,000 is worth £110,000; if you don't take your profit in the form of income you can sell all your units without any CGT liability by soaking up your annual CGT allowance of £10,100 and shortly after reinvest your £110,000. Obviously you don't want to switch out of a perfectly good fund purely for tax reasons, plus, of course, there may well be some dealing costs involved, but it is another tax saving strategy that you should be aware of.

Offshore Investment Bonds

We're not talking palm trees and piña coladas; it doesn't have to be anywhere more exotic than the Isle of Man to enjoy all the tax benefits of being offshore. The Isle of Man has an investor protection regime comparable with that of the UK mainland, is no more complicated to deal with than any part of the UK, plus if you want to visit your investment you won't get sunstroke.

Investment Bonds, offshore or not, permit a basic rate taxpayer to withdraw up to 5% of their initial investment amount for up to 20 years on what is known as a tax-deferred basis. From a tax perspective this is considered a return of your own capital (5% x 20 = 100%) and therefore there are no immediate tax consequences for you. If you want to withdraw more than 5% you may well have a tax liability on the amount above 5%. To calculate the tax liability we need to undertake a calculation which we won't get into here but offshore Bonds can still prove beneficial regardless of your tax rate.

Investing offshore shelters your investment from tax so that you do not have the tax drag on investment growth of losing up to 20% each year in tax so your fund will roll up at a greater rate than the same investment held within the UK (and many Bond funds can be held onshore or offshore that are identical in their makeup).

Offshore funds do come with an additional layer of administration which in turn increases the cost, but very often these can be offset by the tax advantages as you can manage when and where you choose to bring your funds back onshore. Your investment is a ship that remains at sea until you call it ashore and until then no UK taxes are payable. You can decide when and where your investment ship unloads its investment cargo to minimize your income tax liability such as a year when you can reduce your income to below your current tax rate threshold.

Even if you undertake no tax management strategies whatsoever, with your offshore Bond you have the comfort that you can withdraw 5% a year, regardless of the size of your initial investment, for 20 years which should take care of a substantial part of your retirement. To make this option even more attractive there are investment Companies that will now guarantee you a minimum return each year without eroding your capital, so you may enjoy the benefits of a tax-free income in the knowledge that your underlying capital remains safe.

There are also offshore Bonds that not only guarantee you a minimum level of income and capital protection, your income also has the potential to increase over the years. Not for everybody, not least as we are talking a long-term commitment, but from a tax-planning perspective worth more than a little contemplation.

You cannot control or manage inflation but you can arrange some protection against it if you wish. If you cannot avoid income tax on your Pension income you can certainly mitigate it. For all your other retirement income paying tax is surely a voluntary arrangement you choose to make. Inflation and tax is the two-headed Hydra that attacks your standard of living in retirement but even a modest amount of tax planning creates options to improve your income levels without necessarily incurring any additional risk to your capital long term.

11 If you enjoy a gamble

Why Annuities are good for you

Annuities have formed the mainstay of Pension income planning for as long as there have been Pensions and they still provide the largest amount of Pension income, accounting for some 80% of all new Pension income plans. They are a simple, straightforward income provider with a bundle of excellent qualities that will dovetail perfectly with many people's retirement income goals.

Nevertheless, the retirement income market is constantly evolving new and more complex products, not all of them are necessarily for the better as very often a conventional Annuity will fit the bill but it is important that you are aware of what the market has to offer. Many of the plus points of an Annuity can just as easily be interpreted as negative points if you're looking at them from the other direction, not least an Annuity is usually fixed for life, which can be both desirable and undesirable in equal measure.

Let's be sure you understand exactly what an Annuity is

Apart from being the most popular way to take benefits from a Pension, Annuities are also the simplest to understand. You are exchanging your Pension fund with an insurance Company in return for a guarantee that it will pay you an income for the rest of your life.

An Annuity works like a loan in reverse, except the loan you make to the Annuity provider will never be repaid, once you have paid your fund to an insurance Company that's it. You will never see your capital again and in return they will pay you interest for the rest of your life. In addition to the personal factors documented below, Annuity rates are determined by the bigger economic picture relating to interest rates and the yield on 15-year Government Gilts, which in turn are determined by Government spending, inflation and the health of our relationship with the world economy.

So way too many factors for us to influence, but what has made a marked difference to Annuity rates in recent years has been the era of low inflation and low interest rates, which has led to the belief that Annuity rates are poor value as you risk being locked in for life at a 'low' rate. This needs to be placed in the current economic context.

The other factor placing continual downward pressure is of course increasing longevity (we're back to Queen Victoria and her telegrams again!). The longer the insurance Companies estimate they are going to have to pay you for, the lower that income is going to be. Between 1990 and 2007 the lifespan estimates for people retiring at age 60 have increased by 5 years, raising the average retirement span to almost 30 years, an increase of 15% more life which effectively means 15% less income.

More stringent EU regulations are also forcing Annuity providers to hold more Government Gilts rather than Corporate Bonds to reduce their exposure to risk. This has the effect of reducing investment returns and suppressing Annuity rates even further. Overall it is very difficult to see a positive future for Annuity rates with so many forces rallied against them and there is nothing to say that Annuity rates could not fall further.

The rate is one element of the gamble with Annuity purchase, if you wait and Annuity rates rise in the interim you win with a higher income for life, but if rates fall before you buy you are facing a lower income than you might otherwise have enjoyed. For many this debate is academic as there is an urgent need to buy an Annuity at retirement to provide an income and the purchaser has no choice but to accept the prevailing rate when they retire.

Personal Factors

Your age and life expectancy

The older you are when you buy an Annuity the fewer years the insurance Company will expect to have to pay you a Pension, so your income will be approximately 10% higher at age 65 than it would have been at age 60 for the same size fund. The other key factor of which we are already aware is increasing longevity, which is good news unless you are in the Annuity business. Insurance Companies are forever playing catch up as our average life expectancy continues to rise and Actuaries are attempting to second-guess the future. One thing that is absolutely certain is that as longevity improves, Annuity rates will fall correspondingly and as this inevitably continues it can only have a downward impact on income from Annuities, regardless of any other influencing factors.

Gender

Women enjoy longer lives on average than men, although the gap is closing, so an insurance Company would expect to pay an Annuity for more years to a woman than a man of the same age. The initial Pension for a woman at retirement will therefore be less, approximately 5% less, than that of a man of the same vintage with the same size fund.

The projected life expectancy for those aged 65 in 2008 was 17.5 years for men and 20.2 years for women (ONS Interim Life Tables) so if you are female you can expect lower Annuity rates and a lower resulting income in the majority of cases. The exception is where all or part of your fund is made up of protected rights, these accrue from National Insurance Rebates being paid into your fund as a result of being contracted out, then special rules apply, one of which is that Annuities are quoted on a unisex basis.

Lifestyle

Smoking is not usually considered a lifestyle benefit but if you enjoy the occasional puff you will be made extra welcome by Annuity providers as smokers on average tend to inhale for the final time 5 years before non-smokers. This results in a superior Annuity rate for nicotine addicts as the Annuity provider will not, on average, have to pay for as long.

If you have ever been tempted to begin a relationship with the evil weed then now is the time. Although a word of warning, please don't be tempted for that relationship to last only as long as it takes you to fill in your Annuity application as many people have been tempted to do. The insurance Company may well ask you to undergo a test to confirm there is nicotine in your system, or they will write to your GP for confirmation of your smoking habits. If there is any doubt as to your enthusiasm for tobacco, your application for a smoker's rate will be declined. By declaring yourself a smoker if you are not, you may well have committed an act of fraud on the Annuity application, something which insurance Companies take a dim view of so they now maintain a central register of those individuals who have been somewhat poetic in their dealings with them.

If you feel like celebrating your retirement with a bottle of your favourite alcoholic beverage, go right ahead with your Annuity provider's blessing. As with smoking, drinking is a positive lifestyle choice when it comes to buying an Annuity. The number of units of alcohol you consume can have a positive bearing and the greater your fondness for a tipple, the better Annuity rate you will receive. You may smugly toast your passion for vintage burgundies, real ale or whatever your chosen poison is, happy in the knowledge that you will now be getting paid extra as compensation for having a hangover.

A postcode lottery?

It is an oft-quoted tabloid cliché in relation to a number of health issues, but in this instance it's absolutely true. Your postcode will determine the Annuity rate you are offered by insurance Companies who are using ever-more sophisticated social profiling software that can tell them not only what your favourite brand of yoghurt is but actually when you are going to pop your clogs. Slightly scary, but not really that groundbreaking.

We've known for a long time that if you live in Newcastle the chances are you will expire before your counterparts in Kensington for reasons we are all familiar with (hard graft, too many nights on the Quayside etc). These latest techniques are simply refining this concept and developing it into what is fast being regarded as a science. This can of course work in your favour, if you are smoking 40 Regal and drinking 20 pints a day while living in Kensington. Conversely the system will punish you if you happen to be a non-drinker living in Newcastle, an unlikely scenario I concede. However, Annuity providers are refining their longevity predictions to such a degree that is possible to be living on different sides of the same street and be quoted different Annuity rates.

Your good health

Without doubt the biggest factor that will influence your personal Annuity rate is the state of your health. Increasingly Annuities are being 'underwritten' in the same way as life assurance policies have always been, to take account of any health factors that may influence your lifespan. These 'impaired life' Annuities now account for 25% of the Annuity market and are growing in number every year.

If you are in ill health this can result in a substantially higher Annuity rate and therefore a greater income in, what is predicted to be, a shorter retirement. This can incorporate anything that could potentially reduce your life expectancy including medical conditions, family history or what you did for a living.

Medically there are a whole list of very obvious conditions such as cancer, heart disease and diabetes and then a whole lot of less obvious ones so be sure you make very full disclosure on your Annuity application about the parlous state of your physical wellbeing. The closer you are to death's door, ideally pushing right against it, the better Pension income you will get.

Taking into account all the above factors, Annuity providers will arrive at what they consider an appropriate Annuity rate for someone of your circumstances. The other side of the Annuity contract, which determines how much you will actually get paid, is determined by factors that you are in control of and will depend upon your personal requirements.

The type of Pension you want

You have the choice of adding various options to your Pension Annuity at outset. These options will affect your lifetime income and all come at a cost, so once again there is an element of gambling involved, consequently some shrewd conclusions have to be reached.

Providing for your Spouse

Your Pension Annuity can continue to be paid to your Spouse if you predecease them and you have options in respect of the level of Pension you would like them to have. This is expressed as a percentage of your Pension from 100% (so they receive the same amount as you!) 66% or 50% of your Annuity income. The cost of this benefit will be a key factor in reaching your decision so to provide you with an indication:

> A 100% Spouse's Pension will reduce your income from outset by approx 15%
>
> A 66% Spouse's Pension will reduce your income from outset by approx 11%
>
> A 50% Spouse's Pension will reduce your income from outset by approx 8%

So, as a 65-year-old man with a 62-year-old wife you choose to include a 50% Spouse's Pension therefore your initial £10,000 income will reduce to £9,200. The Annuity provider now has to pay this until the last of the two of you die, therefore extending the payment term potentially by several years. The gamble for you is that you purchase a Spouse's Pension and then your Spouse dies first or you divorce, then you have forgone all those years of an additional 8% income paying for a benefit that will never be received. The Annuity provider wins.

You need to take into account your Spouse's age because the younger they are the more expensive it will be to purchase their Pension as the Annuity provider will have to pay them for longer. Providing a 50% Spouse's Pension, if the wife was 50 rather than 60 would reduce the initial Pension by 13% rather than 8%, quite a price to pay. If your Spouse or partner is substantially younger it may not even be possible to obtain a Spouse or partner's Pension at any price.

Perhaps the key determinant in your decision will be the level of need for your Spouse. Are there any significant health issues or family history which might suggest that you may outlive your Spouse? Do they have sufficient Pension income in their own right? What level of State Pension are they entitled to? How significant is the proposed Annuity in the overall income picture? What other assets do they have? Will there be a substantial reduction in their income requirements after your death?

A large number of unknowns to consider, and as with so many Annuity-related decisions it is one that is irrevocable so requires best use of your crystal ball gazing skills.

If you have no Spouse or civil partner none of this is an option, you cannot provide a Pension for anyone else such as children or leave your fund to a good cause, your Pension effectively dies with you, unless of course you pay for some form of capital protection or guarantee.

Annuity guarantees and value protection

One of the most common and justified complaints about Annuities is that, should you die early in retirement, the insurance Company providing your Annuity wins and you and your estate loses. One way to mitigate this potential loss is to purchase a guarantee.

A guarantee provides that should you die during the guaranteed period, which is normally 5 or 10 years, the balance of any payments due would be paid to your dependants or your estate.

For example, you purchase a 5-year guarantee and die 2 years into retirement your estate will receive your Pension payments for a further 3 years and then cease. If you purchase a 10-year guarantee very often the balancing payments due are paid out as a lump sum and thereafter all payments cease. Guarantees in my opinion offer good value, if you purchase a 5-year guarantee it will reduce your Annuity rate by approximately 0.03%, a 10-year guarantee by 0.07% – something that I think is worth investigating if you don't want your major beneficiary to be an insurance Company.

Alternatively you may now purchase a 'value protected' Annuity offering a lump sum death benefit of the Annuity purchase price less the Pension income paid out to date (minus a tax charge). If preferred, a lower percentage of the Annuity value could be protected to provide a balance between your income needs and your understandable desire to leave your Pension fund to your beneficiaries.

Protecting your income against the silent assassin

Polish that crystal ball again, you need to make another decision about the future. What do you think the rate of inflation is going to be over the next 20 years? Impossible to call of course but you can be sure there will be some. Even in the current 'low' inflation environment it has averaged around 2.5% over the last 10 years which has eroded the spending power of £1,000 down to £796, so even a modest amount of this 'low' inflation is going to put a dent into your standard of living in retirement. If we get back to the days of 10% per year inflation, and don't rule anything out, it happened during the 1980s, our notional £1,000 would only be worth £387 in 10 years' time and in 20 years a derisory £135.

If you elect to draw a level Pension, which is not an unreasonable idea, as the State Pension is index linked, you could structure your other investments to provide some protection against inflation. How much better off will you be in the short term?

If you want to purchase an Annuity that increases at 3% per annum that inflation protection benefit will reduce your initial income by around a third, so it will be in the region of 17 years before your income reaches the level you would have had from the start with a level Annuity and more than 25 years before you break even in respect of total income received so index linking is very much a long-term bet. Plus of course if you elect for a level Annuity you have had the use of that additional level Pension income for 20 years or more before you even begin to feel the real benefit of index linking.

Once again this is a decision that is all part of the Annuity gamble, and one where I believe the odds are stacked against you, although I don't want you to get the impression that I think Annuities are a bad idea. I think Annuities are a fantastic concept but I want you to appreciate their limitations.

In fact, Annuities are an absolutely superb product, what other product will pay you a guaranteed, rock solid 100% certain income for your entire life, and that of your Spouse if you wish? Well, apart from Variable Annuities which we will look at in a later chapter, virtually no other retirement income product can offer you such security.

If you live to be 120-years old that Annuity will just keep on paying month after month after month after month. Disregarding the complexities of how Annuities are priced, mortality credit and other dark arts of the Actuarial profession, in simple terms if you are getting 6.5% a year by your 16th year of retirement you have had your money back and are then running at a theoretical profit. If you die before that 16th year of course it is less of a good deal!

Before we get into more depth about the ever-growing variety of Annuities, let's first list the upside and downside of a Conventional Annuity as we have been describing above.

Cheers for Annuities

- ✓ Guaranteed income – it will never fall
- ✓ Simplicity - you pay them then they pay you. Done.
- ✓ No investment risk
- ✓ Security for life
- ✓ Immediate access to all your tax-free cash sum
- ✓ Depending on how long you live, you may get back more than you used to buy the Annuity
- ✓ Enhanced rates available due to lifestyle and health factors

Fears for Annuities

- ✖ You make a decision about your retirement now which you and your family are committed to for the rest of your life – and beyond!
- ✖ You may find that you would have been better off waiting - Annuity rates may rise.
- ✖ Lack of flexibility, whatever your income is you're stuck with it
- ✖ You give up the right to your capital forever

- Lack of options for death benefits
- Your circumstances may change e.g. you may choose to provide benefits for your Spouse and they predecease you
- Inflation may erode the value of your benefits
- If you die soon after the plan has started the payments received may be smaller than the amount invested in the Annuity
- You may not need the same level of income at 90 as you did at 60.

Open market option. What's that about then?

As you approach your selected retirement date your Pension provider may well write to you illustrating the various ways you can take your Pension: tax-free cash/no tax-free cash, inflation-protected or not, Spouse's benefit or not and most importantly what level of income you are likely to receive for the rest of your life.

The Pension quoted is based on your Pension Company's own Annuity rates which may or may not be the best on offer. You should not accept these rates without first asking an IFA to research the market to locate the best rate for you. Remember this is a once-in-a-lifetime decision, and if you just accept the rate offered by your existing Company you may be giving away thousands of pounds of income. Not only are you likely to obtain a better rate, if you get your Annuity application underwritten you may be able to obtain an enhanced rate too. By moving your Pension fund to another provider with a superior rate you are exercising your right to an open market option.

To get an idea of what is on offer there are several Annuity rate comparison websites including the Government-funded www.moneymadeclear.org.uk, but please do not forget money made clear, like so many comparison sites, only carries a selection of Annuity providers, very few encompass the whole market.

If you believe you may have an opportunity to achieve a better Annuity rate on medical grounds, comparison sites are largely meaningless as the Annuity income you receive will ultimately be an underwriting decision based upon your personal circumstances. Don't be seduced by the online discount Annuity providers, this is a once-in-a-lifetime opportunity so it is well worth paying a fee if necessary to ensure you have the best possible rate.

What we have covered above is known as a 'conventional' Annuity but this simple product has begun to mutate into ever-more sophisticated subspecies. This has provided investors with more choice, which is to be welcomed, but also ever-more complexity which can sometimes cause confusion. The word 'Annuity' suggests an air of comfortable certainty, but once we move away from the basic model this is not always the case.

Unit-linked Annuities

These are similar to conventional Annuities in that you can choose for the Annuity to continue after your death to your Spouse and choose a guaranteed period. However, unlike conventional Annuities the level of lifetime income is not guaranteed, but is linked to the performance of an underlying investment in which your Annuity funds have been placed.

You choose an initial level of income that is linked to an anticipated growth rate that you select at outset. The higher the anticipated growth rate, the greater the level of risk. Your future income could be higher or lower than your initial income depending on the performance of your funds in relation to the selected anticipated growth rate.

As your income fluctuates it could be difficult to budget, and your future prosperity could depend on the performance of the underlying funds. This is a higher-risk Annuity option, albeit one with the potential upside of an increasing income.

With-profits Annuities

Unlike conventional Annuities where your income level is guaranteed from outset, the income from with-profits Annuities is linked to the performance of your Annuity provider's with-profits fund.

The with-profits approach is less volatile than the unit-linked option but does still have potential for higher income in the future as the underlying fund will normally have a less-aggressive investment strategy.

Assuming a predetermined rate of growth is achieved on the with-profits fund, income from your with-profits Annuity will be higher than under the conventional Annuity route and could increase in future years. If the required growth rate is not achieved your level of income could reduce, even to below what could have been provided by a conventional Annuity.

The with-profits route is more restrictive than the unit-linked option, you have no choice of investment strategy, but the reduced volatility means that your income should fluctuate less but the reduction in risk is in exchange for more modest returns.

Cheers for investment-linked Annuities

- ✓ You have immediate access to all your tax-free cash sum
- ✓ You may get more back than you used to buy the Annuity in the first place
- ✓ The income you receive may rise in the future
- ✓ Your income could rise in excess of inflation
- ✓ You could buy a conventional Annuity in the future

Fears for investment-linked Annuities

- ✗ Your starting income could be lower than a conventional Annuity and may not rise
- ✗ If the set growth rate for the plan is not achieved the income level may fall

- You have to make your choices at outset that cannot be changed
- You retain investment risk
- There are fewer guarantees than the conventional Annuity route

12 Cry freedom!

Income Drawdown: the good, the bad and the slightly ugly

In 1995 a new type of Pension income method was created that allows you to take some or all of your tax-free cash at outset and then drawdown an income from your Pension fund as and when you required it, not too surprisingly this product became known as 'Income Drawdown' and provided a range of options and flexibility not seen before or since.

The confusing bit

In 2006 HMRC declared that from now on this type of Pension would be known as 'Unsecured Pension' and Annuities, for ease of consumer understanding would now be known as 'Secured Pension'. Confused? Yeah me too! So for ease of MY understanding any references in this book to Unsecured Pension or USP means Income Drawdown.

The even-more confusing bit

This distinction is important to bear in mind when considering Variable Annuities (see next chapter) not least because a Variable Annuity is not actually an Annuity at all but an unsecured unit-linked Pension that is actually secured by a guarantee and can be converted into a non-secured Unsecured Pension at anytime or, of course, into a conventional Annuity which are now, as you know, called Secured Pensions. Easy isn't it? Ok let's keep moving while I've still got you.

Income Drawdown explained

Income Drawdown works differently to other retirement options; up to 25% of your Pension fund can still be taken as a tax-free cash lump sum but instead of purchasing an Annuity the remainder of your Pension fund money remains invested in funds of your choice. This is a great way of keeping control of your money, you know exactly how much you have got, how much you can take, you can invest it where you choose and if anything happens to you along the road, it will be there for your loved ones, after the taxman has had his share of course. As the price of freedom is eternal vigilance either you, your Adviser or both have the responsibility of monitoring your Drawdown plan fund to ensure that you don't deplete your fund beyond repair, which is a very real risk.

Income Drawdown is considered a high-risk strategy, as your funds are going to remain exposed to a whole range of investment risks long into your retirement, a price worth paying you may feel for all the freedom it gives, but a decision that requires continual revisiting, on at least an annual basis in my view.

Your initial income level will be set at outset and the maximum you may have is around the same as if you had chosen to purchase a conventional Annuity. Thereafter your income is recalculated every 3 years, based upon your age and fund size. Due to these income reviews it will practically be impossible to have nothing left at all, but like the radioactive half life of uranium, it may go on halving forever but after a while there won't be enough left to blow your socks off.

Having lots of month left at the end of the money is a concern at any time of life, but particularly poignant when you have no way of accumulating any more of it. The Drawdown option needs to be considered as part of your bigger income picture, if every penny you have for your retirement income is in a Drawdown plan you are running with a colossal risk and the older you get the more that risk increases.

If you have other sources of retirement income, your State Pension for a start, you may be willing to embrace the investment risk of Income Drawdown, if not for all of your Pension pot then perhaps for a proportion, and this proportion can be reduced over time by gradually purchasing a series of Annuities. You need to consider just how vital is this level of income over the longer term?

Increasingly people are using their homes to fund their income needs later in life, something that I am sure will become commonplace as those with inadequate Pension provision (which seems just about everyone under 40!) slip gracelessly into retirement.

Remember our U-shaped retirement income curve? What is to stop you using your Pension in Income Drawdown to fund your lifestyle on the left hand side of that U and your home when your income needs begin to climb again up the right hand side of our U? If you feel that you are going to need the highest level of income during the early years of retirement whilst you are fit and well then Income Drawdown is one way to maximize that.

Survey after survey of older people tells the same thing, when asked if they would do anything different the same sentiment comes back time after time; they wish they had taken more risks. I know it's easy for me to say it's not my money, but I meet so many people who were a part of the generation when thrift and prudence were a way of life and they just can't break the habit. I've lost count of the number of times I've had elderly clients tell me, "I've got more than I've ever had and I just can't spend it" or "what use is to me now, I wish I'd had it when I was young."

Naturally as a cool-headed IFA I don't want to be encouraging reckless behaviour but you've spent your life earning it, saving it and probably a good deal of the time lying awake worrying about it, so why not have a plan to spend it? That probably was your intention when you started out.

Flexibility and control of such a strategy can provide a varying income, within limits, to draw as and when you please while protecting your residual fund for your family or others when you die – but it cannot be done without risk.

So book that cruise and prepare for future worst; you are taking maximum income, the stock market crashes repeatedly and bad investment decisions are taken. You know your money is finite but you are having a review every year so you know exactly where you are. At least there are going to be no nasty surprises when you get to 75 by which time you're virtually running on empty. Along the way you have been developing a contingency plan, this could involve using a portion of your fund to buy an Annuity to cover essentials, other investments, downsizing or equity-releasing your house, even simply slowing down your rate of spending. Everyone's retirement strategy will incorporate different amounts of diverse ingredients so the recipe will be unique, just as long as you end up with an income cake big enough to take different size slices to satisfy your changing appetite.

Real life...

My client Jim: "I love the freedom the Drawdown thing can give me and the fact that my fund can go to my kids when I fall off my perch but I really can't be doing with worrying about investment risk at my age so just stick my fund in cash and I'll live on the interest for now and see how it goes."

Not really a strategy that is going to work in the longer term, you are making 4% interest but our old adversary inflation will be doing its worst, plus you will have the cost of running your Drawdown plan of 1%-2% a year as we poor Advisers can't live on fresh air, then when you do want to start taking a realistic level of income you are going to have to either take greater risks when you are older or you are going to have to transfer into something else and incur additional cost. Sitting in cash is not a strategy for Drawdown. You need to look at other investment options and this is why you have to be comfortable with investment risk.

MY FINANCIAL BELIEFS MIGHT SEEM UNORTHODOX, BUT MY LUCKY BLACK INVESTMENT RAT NEVER FAILS TO WARN ME WHEN TO LEAVE THE SINKING SHIP

How much income can I have in Drawdown?

You are obliged to take an income directly from your Pension fund each year which is taxed at source like PAYE as earned income. The income taken must fall between limits set by The Government Actuaries Department. These limits and therefore the amount you may take as income are reviewed every 3 years and amended in line with Annuity rates at that time. Linked to Annuity rates, Drawdown rates increase with age so you will be entitled to a greater percentage of your fund as income at age 70 than you are at 60. These limits are set so as to reduce the chances of you running out of money and then becoming reliant upon the State.

As your personal income parameters are set for 3 years at outset as a numeric figure, which is in pounds and pence rather than as a percentage of your fund. Regardless of whether your fund doubles in value or halves in value during the following 3-year period your income limits will be unchanged during that time.

You can vary your income within your annual limits as often as you wish, the only thing to remember is that if you elect not to take your income in a particular year it cannot be 'rolled over' to the following year, so if you take nothing this year you cannot take twice the amount next year.

Real life…

Mike is 60 and has three personal Pensions and two Company schemes he has built up over a lifetime of employment. After discussions Mike decides he has three real priorities:

He wants everything in one place for simplicity, he wants to be able to vary his income and most importantly he wants to be able to leave his Pension fund to his disabled daughter. We agree that Income Drawdown is the way forward and after transferring his entire fund into a Drawdown contract he has a total of £132,000. Mike takes his maximum tax-free cash of £33,000 and we calculate that he can take anywhere between zero and £7,128 as an annual income.

Mike decides that he doesn't need any income in the first year but after a couple of months chooses to take a one-off payment of £2,500 for an unforeseen expense. In the second year he takes nothing, allowing his fund to build up and at the start of the third year he takes his maximum annual income as a single payment, with a view to commence monthly payments at the end of year 3. Meanwhile the 'income' he hasn't taken is growing in his underlying funds and will improve his chances of an increased income at his first 3-year review.

What happens if you die in Drawdown?

One of the biggest complaints about Pensions come from single people, who may be single because they have never married, they are divorced or widowed. Whatever the reason many of them face the same irritating scenario for their Pension if they die, it dies with them. You may have worked somewhere near 40 years and accrued a Pension worth hundreds of thousands of pounds, but the minute you expire so can your Pension and if this happens early in retirement it is particularly punitive. Income Drawdown allows you to largely avoid this scenario because if you die in Drawdown and are married or in a civil partnership your other half has three options:-

1. Take the Pension fund as a cash lump sum (subject to a tax charge of 55%)

2. Buy an Annuity with the remaining fund.

3. Continue to take Income Drawdown. (After 2 years the income limits are recalculated to your surviving partner's age).

If you are single your Pension fund is returned to your estate (subject to tax naturally) and distributed in line with your wishes, to children, grandchildren or the stray dogs home, if that's your choice.

Real life...

Bob had worked for the Civil Service for 37 years, his Pension was simply as good as it gets so when he came to see me 1 year before he was due to retire saying he felt he should transfer into Income Drawdown I politely suggested that he may wish to take a lie down in a darkened room until the feeling passed. He pointed out that, as a divorcee with two grown-up daughters, when he died his Pension would die with him and he wanted to leave whatever was left of his Pension to his daughters. Bob's view was that no matter how reckless his Drawdown strategy it would always be more than the big fat zero the Civil Service Pension would leave behind.

How many more Bobs are there out there? Millions possibly. How many should be leaving quality Company Pension schemes to go into Drawdown? Very few, but it's another example of everyone having different priorities, not a matter of right or wrong answers.

So it's all good news then?

An attraction of Drawdown is the potential for an ever-rising income, but this is also where it can get slightly ugly. Putting it simply if your underlying fund is growing faster than what you are drawing as an income which is capped by the Government, you will be forever running at a profit and each 3-year review will see your income rising accordingly.

So with all the choice and flexibility and not least the possibility of an increasing income why doesn't everyone go into Income Drawdown? When it works well it is an extremely successful strategy, but when it doesn't things can look very bleak. The success of Income Drawdown is contingent upon your investment strategy and very often this can be affected by events that are way out of your control, such as the collapse of world markets in 2008. Let's look at a hypothetical scenario but one that many people who have been in Drawdown over the last 10 years will recognize.

Below we are showing the returns on two £100,000 portfolios started 20 years ago to provide income for our two clients, Mr Grey and Mr Black. Both clients viewed themselves as high-risk investors and as you can see they have enjoyed mixed fortunes, with some years producing +30%, others showing falls of -20%, but overall was this a successful strategy for Income Drawdown?

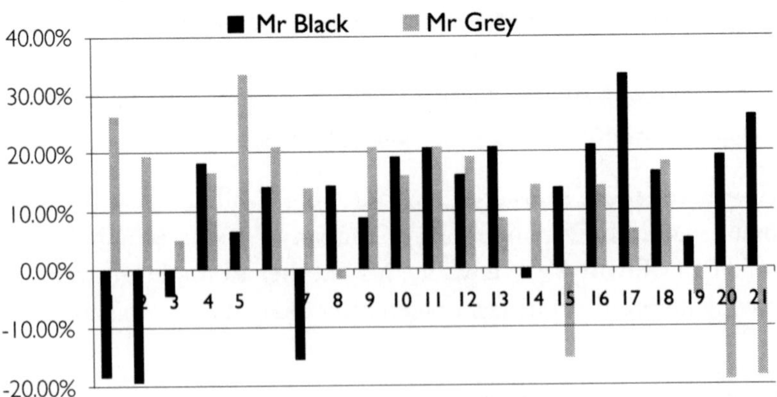

Both Mr Grey and Mr Black have been drawing £5,000 income increasing at 3.5% per annum and have been taking it annually in advance.

The average annual return on both portfolios has been 10.39% so what are their portfolios now worth?

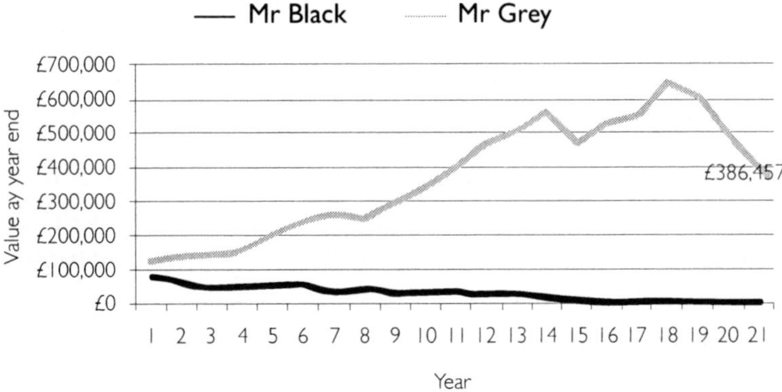

As you can see Mr Grey is enjoying a comfortable retirement, Mr Black is penniless. Why?

The sequence of return

In the graph on the page opposite the total returns over time are exactly the same; the Grey portfolio is actually the change in the value of the FTSE100 over 21 years. The Black portfolio is the same index but the years and therefore the returns have been reversed. Whilst both investors have experienced exactly the same returns it is the sequence of those returns that has been crucial to the outcome. A couple of bad years for Mr Black to start with and he never recovers, a couple of good years for Mr. Grey and he has momentum to sustain him through the bad times. It is not just returns that matter, it is the sequence of return – something we have limited control of and certainly no way of predicting.

Even if Mr Black had been on the positive side, let's not forget that charges also have to be deducted that will normally be 1%-2% every year which will compound any investment problems even further. As we saw in an earlier example, sitting in cash is not a feasible option for Drawdown but if your fund falls 25% in value as many peoples' did during 2008, and you continue to withdraw maximum income, the effect on your fund can be terminal.

Let's say we agree a level of income at outset which we know your fund can withstand based on a number of reasonable assumptions, then along comes an unplanned event, it doesn't have to be anything as dramatic as the collapse of capitalism, a simple fall in the market or a typhoon in Taiwan and potentially you have a long-term income problem.

Your short-term income requirements are unlikely to diminish but your fund may do and instead of relying on growth to provide you with an income you are now having to dig into your invested capital. Your residual fund is then going to have to work even harder which in turn means taking more risk and then any further falls will be more dramatic. The negative yield spiral continues until you are left with a greatly depleted fund and ever-diminishing options. At any point you can decide enough is enough and run into the secure and reassuring arms of an Annuity, but it will be for a much-reduced income and one that in all probability will never increase.

This is the nightmare scenario which for many people can become all too real. So whilst Income Drawdown can in many ways be the answer to all your retirement income prayers it is a high risk strategy and you need to be prepared for all the potential outcomes. We all hope to have an income like Mr Grey, but don't rule out the possibility of becoming Mr Black.

Cheers for Income Drawdown

- ✓ Allows you to receive all of your tax-free cash as a lump sum or in stages if preferred
- ✓ Income can be varied within the income limits which may assist in tax planning
- ✓ With good investment performance your Pension income can keep increasing indefinately
- ✓ Annuity purchase can be postponed, permanently if you wish
- ✓ On your death your family can benefit from the value of your Pension fund (minus tax)
- ✓ You remain in control of your Pension fund
- ✓ Maximum investment choice

Fears for Income Drawdown

- ✗ There is no guarantee that your income will ultimately be as high as a conventional Annuity
- ✗ Annuity rates may decrease in the future making Annuity purchase more expensive
- ✗ The value of funds remaining invested in your Pension will fluctuate
- ✗ If your Pension fund does not grow sufficiently your future income may have to reduce
- ✗ Your fund could be eroded over time leaving you with very little income
- ✗ There are costs for fund management and ongoing reviews
- ✗ A combination of high withdrawals and poor investment performance could reduce your fund and income virtually to nothing
- ✗ Poor investment returns in the early years could derail your entire retirement income strategy

13 The road to Shangri La

Guarantees, income and Variable Annuities

The 'G' word is always attractive and never more so than in the world of investment. True guarantees are extremely valuable, and one of the first questions you may want to ask yourself as you approach retirement is 'how much of my retirement income do I want to be guaranteed?'

Your initial answer to that question may be '100% of course!' but when you begin to look at what is actually offered with a guarantee you may not be quite so enthusiastic.

You know Annuities are guaranteed and you are aware of the constraints that apply to them, but let's take a quick look at some examples of what is to be had both in and outside of Pension plans, remembering the clear relationship between risk and reward.

NS&I

National Savings and Investments products are all guaranteed as they are underwritten by the Government, so the lowest risk investment provides the lowest reward, with 5-year Bonds very often offering rates around the rate of inflation and less than you could obtain on the High Street, although NS&I products are often tax free.

Index-linked certificates, if available, will provide a compound return of the inflation rate plus 1% over periods of 5 years. Income Bonds are even less generous, currently paying 2% per annum and subject to income tax.

Building society Bonds

With a range of terms and rates they do offer some protection for your cash against inflation, but once you have allowed for income tax you will be unlikely to make much of a return, in real terms anything over 1% could be considered a success. These types of accounts are known as savings rather than investments with very good reason, but they are relatively safe as your capital is guaranteed up to £85,000 for each institution you hold an account with.

Unit trusts/Open-ended Investment Companies (OEICs)

Any unit trust or OEIC has the potential to provide you with an income but the two principal sectors which do this are Corporate Bond and Equity Income.

Corporate Bonds are issued in return for loans investors have made to Companies and the interest on those loans can be paid in the form of income. A Corporate Bond OEIC may hold 30-40 different Companies' Bonds with varying rates of interest and maturity dates. Corporate Bonds are issued by Companies with diverse financial standing. These Bonds may be so-called 'investment grade' from blue chip Companies offering lower rates of interest right along the spectrum to high-risk Companies whose future is uncertain and whose debt is referred to rather disparagingly as junk Bonds.

Equity Income funds focus on shares that pay dividends to provide you with an income, and as these tend to be more mature and stable Companies they are not perhaps as risky as a UK All Companies stock market fund, but nevertheless they will rise and fall in value. Of course, one of the key concepts behind them is that as the value of the underlying shares held in your chosen fund can appreciate in value, so therefore does the value of your investment and, over time, your income.

IT CAME TO ME
IN THE LAUNDERETTE
MEMO
SHARES MAY
GO UP, DOWN
AROUND AND
AROUND OR
SHRINK OUT
OF ALL
PROPORTION

Variable Annuities

As you have seen previously, conventional Annuities come with a healthy list of advantages, not least that they can provide you with a secure income guaranteed for life. Major downsides include the fact that it will die with you and even if you elect for an inflation-protected Annuity your spending power is never going to increase in real terms, nor do you have no flexibility to fine tune your Annuity as your circumstances and aspirations change. At the other end of the Pension spectrum Income Drawdown gives you maximum flexibility and the potential for a rising income, but not without significant risk. It is between these two polar opposites that the so-called 'Variable Annuity' comes into its own.

Like so many financial planning ideas the Variable Annuity has made its way across the Atlantic, they are widely sold in the North American Pensions market attracting $150 billion each and every year into a market already estimated to be worth a $1 trillion. So what's the huge attraction? Ostensibly you have the best of all worlds – a guaranteed and potentially rising income, flexibility and a range of death benefit options. So what exactly is a Variable Annuity?

Calling it an Annuity might be OK in the USA but to us on this side of the pond it is slightly confusing because it strongly resembles an

Income Drawdown plan accompanied by certain guarantees. The word variable refers to the fact that it can move up or down in value depending upon the performance of the underlying investments which could be in the stock market or Bonds. The Annuity element is more obvious to understand; you will be paid a fixed amount for a fixed term regardless of any underlying investment conditions.

Variable Annuity providers initially sought to address the traditional concern about buying Annuities, namely that if the purchaser dies during the early years they lose out. By offering guaranteed death benefits the annuitant's estate is sure of receiving a guaranteed level of benefit. This concept was extended and Variable Annuities providers began offering 'living' guarantees in addition to those payable upon death.

The first Variable Annuity arrived in the UK around 10 years ago; the Annuity Growth Account from Canada Life is a combination of a 5-year Annuity and a unit-linked investment. The Annuity payable is the same as a conventional Annuity from Canada Life, but because it only has to be paid for 5 years the cost is much less, leaving the larger remaining portion of your Pension fund to be invested for 5 years, at which time you will have the option to purchase a Lifetime Annuity or repeat the process for another 5 years. The concept was simple, you retained some flexibility and if your fund grows during the 5-year period so does your future income plus you always have the option to transfer somewhere else at the end of each 5-year period.

Variable Annuities have grown increasingly sophisticated since then and there are now several providers in the UK offering a menu of capital and income guarantees, including a guaranteed level of income at some point in the future so you can plan ahead with confidence. There are also various death-benefit guarantees that mean you can be sure of leaving a certain amount of capital or income for your nearest and dearest if that is a priority.

Living-benefit guarantees can take a variety of forms, providing a guaranteed capital sum at a given date in the future, a guaranteed level of income immediately or one commencing at an agreed future date. Triggering the income guarantee is similar to purchasing an Annuity as the income benefit is then locked in, providing the comfort of a minimum level of income over your lifetime. These guarantees can also assure you or your beneficiaries of a minimum amount of payments, regardless of your individual lifespan.

In recent years we have witnessed growing consumer demand for protected investments in the face of falling stock markets and that has seen a number of so-called ratchet or step-up guarantees coming on the market so that you can share in any investment growth without the risk of loss. It is this protection from market risk that allows holders of Variable Annuities to sleep at night and is extremely attractive for anyone seeking capital growth or a predictable income stream without the fear of being trapped in the vortex of a plummeting stock market.

There are certain similarities to a conventional Annuity in that you pay your fund across in return for a guaranteed income for life, but usually your Variable Annuity income is less than the open-market conventional Annuity rate. Nevertheless you have the comfort that should your underlying fund rise in value so will your income and once that increase is in place it will be locked in for life.

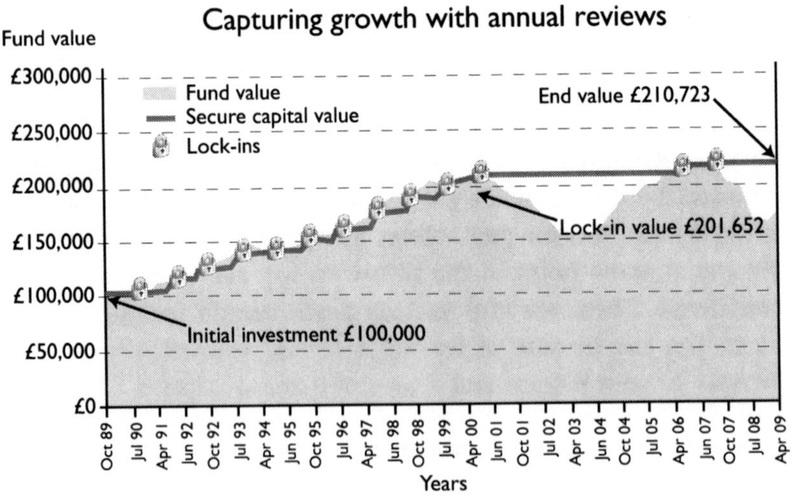

Every year your fund can be reassessed and either your income remains the same for the following 12 months if your fund has experienced no growth or if your fund has grown, so will your income and the value of your underlying fund. It is this ratchet effect on your income that is possibly the biggest attraction of Variable Annuities. You also have the comfort that at any time in the future you can bail out into full-bloodied Income Drawdown or buy a conventional Annuity if you prefer the quiet life.

Although your Variable Annuity fund may well be invested in the stock market and a range of traditionally high-risk areas, you don't care as your fund value is never going to fall – guaranteed. You can greet every stock market crash with a self-satisfied grin and every stock market rise with an even broader grin as you know that your Variable Annuity fund and Pension income are going to be ratcheted up at your next policy anniversary. You get to share in the growth of the assets in your fund without having to share in the losses. So what's the catch?

Like all luxury products it comes at a premium price and you will have to pay what is essentially an insurance premium for the guarantee that can very often be 1% of your fund value per year. There are also limitations on your investment choices and the portfolios offered are usually at the top end of the charge range.

Levels of guaranteed income

Variable Annuities come with a variety of guarantees but at retirement perhaps the most important is the level of guaranteed income. Once you decide to commence drawing an income, the starting level will be determined by your age and be guaranteed for life, regardless of fund performance or how long you live. The guaranteed income levels vary between Companies but to give you an indication here are the actual levels of income currently available from one of the leading Variable Annuity Companies;

	Just you	With Spouse's Option
Age 60	4.0%	3.5%
Age 65	4.25%	3.75%
Age 70	4.5%	4.0%

If you wish to select the Spouse's option, 100% of your guaranteed income will continue to be paid until the second death of yourself and your Spouse and any residual fund can be left to your chosen beneficiaries. The guaranteed income percentage will be based on the lower of you or your Spouse's age at the point income commences.

There are other Variable Annuity products that will pay the maximum income possible as if you were in Income Drawdown so if you are a 65-year-old man you could currently draw an income of approximately 8%, but if you wish to maximize your income then it's a compromise and this would inevitably effect the levels of capital guarantee available to you, once again a question of your own priorities.

The level of guaranteed income is broadly equivalent to index-linked Annuity rates, although positive returns on your underlying investment portfolio will mean your guaranteed income could be stepped up at a rate well above inflation. Of course you could experience several years of flat or falling markets in the early years of retirement so you cannot rely on an increasing income in the same way as if you had purchased an index-linked Annuity.

Additionally you can transfer from your Variable Annuity to another Pension at any time, but the transfer amount could be lower than your guaranteed fund value (for example if you transferred away in October 2003 in the diagram below) so you need to be selective if you choose to do that. You should really regard these types of Annuity as a long-term commitment – possibly even for life, as all the guaranteed benefits will be lost when you transfer away and surrender penalties may apply. Also there is no guarantee that a transfer away will ultimately result in higher retirement benefits for you over the longer term.

In our example below our client has elected to lock in any growth every 2.5 years

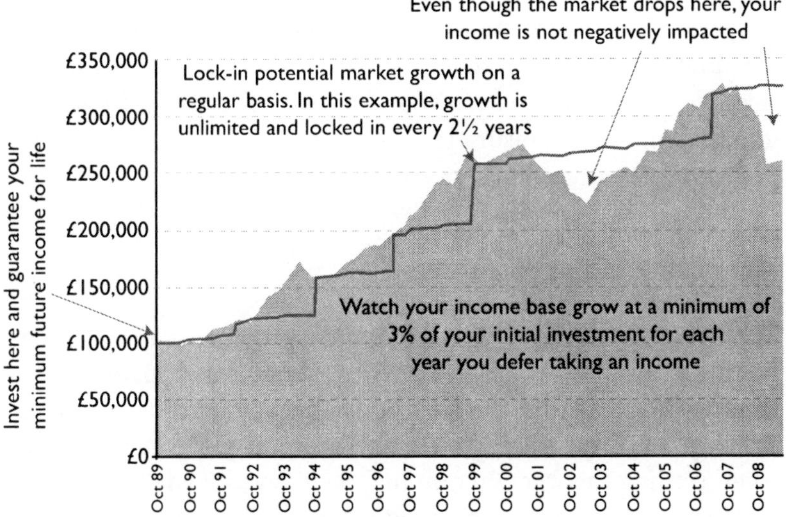
Even though the market drops here, your income is not negatively impacted
Lock-in potential market growth on a regular basis. In this example, growth is unlimited and locked in every 2½ years
Watch your income base grow at a minimum of 3% of your initial investment for each year you defer taking an income
Invest here and guarantee your minimum future income for life
£350,000
£300,000
£250,000
£200,000
£150,000
£100,000
£50,000
£0
Oct 89
Oct 90
Oct 91
Oct 92
Oct 93
Oct 94
Oct 95
Oct 96
Oct 97
Oct 98
Oct 99
Oct 00
Oct 01
Oct 02
Oct 03
Oct 04
Oct 05
Oct 06
Oct 07
Oct 08

Guaranteed lump sums

As well as providing an income your fund can be guaranteed to be a certain value at a chosen maturity date which can be anything from 3-10 years in the future. At that time you can then choose to buy a further Variable Annuity or a different Pension product of your choice depending upon your circumstances at that time. The Guaranteed Maturity Value is calculated to be sufficient to maintain approximately the same level of income after the maturity date as before it, so you will always have an indication of your long-term income while still retaining the option to switch into something else if you wish.

Death benefit options

The facility to purchase a guaranteed income for life for your partner at the start is certainly attractive, but as we know from our stroll around conventional Annuities this can prove an expensive waste of money if your partner predeceases you, so in addition to the standard Spouse's option Variable Annuities can offer you a range of features to protect your investment in the event of death such as a guaranteed minimum lump sum or a guaranteed transfer value for your Spouse or partner to use to their best advantage. If you are single the choice of death benefit options can be particularly valuable as you can ensure your Pension fund doesn't disappear into the coffers of an insurance Company if you are unlucky enough to die early in retirement.

The quality of the guarantee

The attraction of these types of Pension products is that you have no more sleepless nights worrying about investments falling, income dropping and the poorhouse beckoning. But, and it is a sizeable but, these products are only as good as the guarantee and when reading this chapter you may well have asked, 'how can any Company guarantee that my investments will never fall?'

The quality of the underlying guarantee is of course critical to the success of the whole investment strategy and you need to satisfy yourself that your Pension Company will always be in a position to honour their commitment to you. This is largely dependent upon two things: the financial security of the Company issuing your Variable Annuity and the nature of how the underlying guarantee is provided.

The first is far easier to establish than the second which is usually provided by purchasing complex financial contracts called derivatives. These give the purchaser (your Variable Annuity provider) the right to buy or sell certain investments by a predetermined date for an agreed price thereby ensuring the value of the underlying portfolio is guaranteed.

The institution your Pension provider enters into a contract with for these derivatives is known as a counterparty, so the quality of the guarantee is only as good as the quality of the relevant counterparty. Your Adviser needs to make appropriate enquiries to be as sure as they can be that these guarantees will be honoured regardless of investment conditions, so as to minimize what is known in the trade as counterparty risk.

The period from 2008-2010 witnessed the most volatile and illiquid markets we have ever seen and a major milestone was the disappearance of Lehman Brothers, one of the largest providers of these types of counterparty contracts. I am glad to say that there has not been a single instance in the UK Variable Annuity market (or USA for that matter) where a guarantee of this sort has not been honoured. We have been through a truly challenging time for Variable Annuities and their ability to perform has been stretched to the limits, yet they have continued to deliver what they contractually promised. Most importantly people that invested in them have been spectators to the investment carnage that occurred, sitting on the sidelines comfortable in the knowledge that their investment value and in turn their income is never going to fall, and when the markets began to rise so did their portfolio value and lifetime income.

Real life...

Janice was attracted to Income Drawdown, just turned 60 she was working part time, she liked the idea of flexible income and the opportunity to ultimately leave her Pension fund to her children. She knew she had to take risks for Drawdown to work long term but wanted some certainty her bills would be paid. Not remotely excited by the level of Annuity rates on offer we decided to place half her fund in Income Drawdown and half in a Variable Annuity.

Her Income Drawdown plan could provide her with an income of 6.8% per year. Her Variable Annuity could only provide her with a guaranteed 4% for life, but it was safe and had the potential to increase. If she wanted to defer taking her income from her Variable Annuity and wait until she was 65 she could have a guaranteed income for life of 4.89%.

Janice didn't want to wait and went for the 50/50 split as proposed and has an annual income of 5.4% of her fund value with a potential to increase. Also she still retains her options to switch into full Drawdown or purchase an Annuity if she wishes. Plus her remaining fund is preserved for her children.

A menu of options

I believe the main reason for the explosive growth in demand for Variable Annuities is probably the same reason you are reading this book; the desire for more choices within a secure investment environment. With everyone seeking an individual solution to their own personal retirement income problems rather than being presented with a one-size-fits-all solution as so often appears the case with Annuities. The advent of so-called 'living benefits' in the Variable Annuity market provides an abundance of alternatives that we have never previously had available to us, giving us that one thing so many seek in retirement – financial certainty.

There are a whole range of living benefit options that can be mixed and matched to your individual circumstances, whether income or capital guarantees are important, (or both!) death benefits, Spouse's benefits, whatever your priorities, Variable Annuities are proving flexible and adaptable enough to meet the changing and very individual needs of today's Pensioners.

Cheers for Variable Annuities

- ✓ You will never run out of money
- ✓ Your fund is guaranteed not to fall in value regardless of investment conditions
- ✓ The guarantee of an income for life
- ✓ You can provide a specific level of income for your Spouse
- ✓ Worry-free investment portfolios
- ✓ Potential for increasing income every year by sharing in investment growth
- ✓ Flexibility to change your requirements in the future
- ✓ Avoids 'once-in-a-lifetime' commitment of conventional Annuity purchase
- ✓ No commitment or cost to provide for Spouse at outset
- ✓ Capital protection can be built in
- ✓ Various death benefit options

Fears for Variable Annuities

- ✗ All guarantees come at a cost and have to be paid for explicitly
- ✗ Lower income than a conventional Annuity at outset
- ✗ You will not enjoy the full value of any investment growth
- ✗ Investment choices will be limited
- ✗ Fund management charges may be higher than conventional investment funds
- ✗ Charges and surrender values can be prohibitive
- ✗ Variable Annuities are relatively new and some designs are complex
- ✗ The cost of guarantees and other fees put a drag on investment growth
- ✗ There is always counterparty risk
- ✗ If you transfer away any guarantees will be lost

Variable Annuities with guarantees can offer an acceptable compromise between a potentially rising income and security, ensuring that your Pension income stream can be protected and predicted whilst at the same time offering you the opportunity for capital and income growth. Inevitably the cost of the guarantee and other restrictions will place a drag on the underlying investment growth; whether or not this is a price worth paying depends upon your personal priorities and the importance to you of capital security.

The key to perpetuating income and being able to realize your retirement goals is to preserve your capital and a Variable Annuity can help you achieve this. These types of Pension products are very much being promoted as a 'third way', a halfway house between a conventional Annuity and Income Drawdown and whilst no Pension income product will give you everything you want on your wish list, Variable Annuities will probably tick more of your boxes than most and their increasing popularity is easy to understand in these uncertain times.

14 A place in the sun

Pensions and retiring abroad

You wake up with a start. Slowly letting out your breath you realize that strange sound you can hear is the sea. You've retired and the reason it's so light is because this morning, like every morning of your life now, you are awoken by bright sunshine and the only rush you have is to get to the bakers before they run out of fresh bread.

Who hasn't dreamt even briefly of a life in the sun? There are certainly many lifestyle advantages to retiring abroad and there can be advantages financially too, but apart from sunstroke there can be other dangers and serious long-term financial implications you need to consider.

Every country brings its own individual pleasure and challenges and we are not going to dwell on that here. We will however have a canter through some of the key Pension issues in this chapter but this is one area where you really MUST seek professional advice because the wrong decisions or simply believing that things will take care of themselves could prove disastrous for you and your family. Anyway, enough of the doom and gloom, where did I put that sunscreen?

State Pension

The State Pension can be paid to you virtually anywhere in the world so you will have the comfort of knowing that source of income will always be there to provide for the basics in life. One of the main advantages of the State Pension is of course the benefit of annual index linking to protect your income against inflation but this benefit is affected by where you choose to live in the world.

After a lengthy court battle it was finally decided in April 2010 that if you live outside the EU your State Pension will be frozen at the level it was when you left the UK, you will not benefit from any annual index-linked increases. Therefore if you choose to live anywhere in the commonwealth such as Australia or New Zealand you will not enjoy the same Pension rights as someone who chooses to live in France or Spain. Like me, you may have a view on the fairness of such a decision but unfortunately that's the law. I am sure this will not be a deciding factor as to where you choose to spend your retirement, but it could be significant over a 20 or 30-year period as we have already seen the damage that even modest inflation can do to the value of your income. How important is the State Pension to your overall income plan?

The vast majority of countries have agreements with the UK for payment of Pension and other Social Security benefits. If you are going to another country in the EU or a country which has a Social Security agreement with the UK, you might be able to get a benefit which you would not normally get abroad or an individual benefit which that country provides. Full details are available on a country-by-country basis in brochures on the Government's Pensions Service website.

Payments of Pensions can usually be made by BACS transfer to your bank at no cost to you and the taxation position will depend on your residency status and the legislation of the country you are living in. We would strongly recommend that you seek local professional advice to ensure you are compliant with the local tax law to avoid any nasty tax bills in the future.

Payment of Company and Personal Pensions

In the 21st Century, payment of any funds to anywhere in the world should not present a problem and I have not come across a case in recent years where it was not possible to have Pension income paid into a bank account in another country. Inevitably there will be additional bureaucracy involved and it may take time to run smoothly but once your UK Pension provider and the foreign bank get their act together there should not be an issue and in this age of internet banking you should be able to manage the situation quite easily.

I would advise close attention to where your pounds are converted into Euros, Dollars or Baht as you could be paying a commission on conversion and you may be able to obtain a superior exchange rate to the one offered by your bank. There are specialist currency traders that can advise you on this, for example you may be better served receiving your Pension in one annual payment rather than on a monthly basis as charges can amount to a significant reduction in your monthly income and inevitably your lifestyle is going to be at the mercy of currency fluctuations. In extreme cases this could lead to hardship and possibly even repatriation as we have witnessed in recent years as the pound fell against the Euro squeezing thousands of people off the Costas and back to the UK.

Retiring your Pension abroad

It has always been possible to transfer your Pension to another country but is now easier than it has ever been with the advent of QROPS in 2006. Anyone with a UK Pension scheme who now lives, or plans to live, abroad can transfer their existing Pension provision into an overseas Pension scheme known as a QROPS (Qualifying Recognised Overseas Pensions Scheme). The financial benefits can be substantial if planned properly and by planning in advance you could improve the investment growth, flexibility and future financial security of your retirement income, not to mention substantially reduce the tax you pay along the way.

Approximately 200,000 people permanently leave the UK every year and the majority of them will have Pension benefits in some form. Whether you have Personal Pensions, Company benefits or other arrangements there may be a number of reasons to consider taking your Pensions with you.

What exactly are QROPS?

Transfers to an overseas Pension scheme can only take place with Revenue approval and historically this approval effectively eradicated many of the potential tax advantages. Fortunately this position has now changed – for the time being anyway. I personally believe it is only a matter of time before HMRC realizes that they are being far too generous (in their view) and impose tighter restrictions on transfers out of the UK.

A Qualifying Recognised Overseas Pension Scheme (QROPS) as the name suggests, is a Pension based outside the UK that has been approved by HMRC to receive transfers from UK-registered schemes. Due to the substantial tax benefits enjoyed by UK Pensions there are very tight restrictions on the type of plans that receives HMRC approval and can therefore receive transfers. A list of such schemes can be found at http://www.hmrc.gov.uk/PENSIONSCHEMES/qrops-list.htm. There are literally hundreds because as you can appreciate there are an ever-increasing number of Brits who are emigrating, many of them to work in jobs that will offer them a Pension scheme and they want the right to take their UK-accrued Pensions with them.

As well as a lot of the mainstream schemes such as the Australian Nurses Superannuation fund or the Canadian Civil Service Scheme, there are more specialist schemes providing Pensions for those that wish to plan their retirement on an individual basis and the right QROPS will very much depend on your own personal circumstances. QROPS are available in all sorts of exotic locations and it is very important that you seek one registered in a country that has a financial regulatory system as robust as that of the UK to reduce the chances of stepping in any bear traps.

The HMRC list that contains all available QROPS is updated every month. If the Revenue believes a particular QROPS is being used to 'abuse' the UK tax system, approval will be withdrawn. To receive approval from the Revenue (and no UK insurance Company or scheme trustee can transfer funds without this approval), the QROPS must meet certain stringent requirements.

QROPS advice

As with any form of financial advice, we would strongly recommend that you only work with the highest-qualified professionals as this can be an extremely complex area and you don't want any nasty surprises from the Taxman in the future, because wherever you are in the world they all speak the same language.

There are numerous websites offering advice from various European locations claiming to be 'UK registered' or 'UK qualified'. In the same way that appearing on *Crimewatch* does not make you a TV personality, being UK registered does not make you an authorized financial adviser. Make absolutely sure that anyone you deal with is authorised <u>and</u> regulated in the UK and confirm the bona fides on the Register of Financial Advisers at www.fsa.gov.uk.

Also be particularly wary of any fees involved, transferring into a QROPS can prove a complex exercise and anyone offering to do it for £250 is unlikely to be able to offer anything approaching a reasonable service. There are several firms offering what appear to be bargains, simple low-cost QROPS or 'lite' versions of their more expensive big brothers. Be sure these are adequate for your needs or you could end up paying twice when you discover the Pension you have purchased is too restrictive for your needs.

Real life…

Mr Mallaris has £1m in various UK Pensions and is planning to retire to Malta, the country of his birth, so a QROPS is an ideal solution as he doesn't have to draw an income which he doesn't need and when he dies his entire tax-free Pension fund can be passed to his children. Confusing cost with value he opts for the cheapest lite version QROPS, so he will only ever be permitted to invest his Pension fund with one Investment Company at a time.

This not only limits his investment opportunities and creates a huge potential risk to his capital it means his investments are likely to be held in some form of insurance Bond that will give him a reasonable range of funds but they will be more expensive to buy than if he purchased them directly. Also every time he moves between funds he will pay a commission and these commissions will very soon be far greater in total than the fees he would have paid as a one-off cost for establishing a full facility QROPS at outset, which a fund of this size easily justifies.

Avoid the pitfalls of cheap and cheerful but equally be wary of the offshore Pension that can do anything – for a fee! At the other end of the fee scale I am aware of QROPS that charge 9% of your Pension fund for the privilege of transferring to them. Even this exorbitant amount can appear attractive with the seductive promise that you will never have to pay tax again and you can spend your Pension fund on anything you wish as and when you choose. I would love to believe it was true but the cynic inside me just won't let me.

As with all things there is a balance to be found, you do not need to buy a racing yacht if you never plan to leave the harbour, but at the same time don't expect a pedalo to take you around the world. Once again a good Adviser will be able to ascertain your requirements and do research to arrive at a suitably priced QROPS for your needs.

Costs and benefits

In terms of costs these are usually calculated as a percentage of your fund value, the larger your fund the lower the charges will be. Typically your Pension fund needs to be £100,000 but there are schemes available for less than this amount. QROPS are expensive to establish and administer, typically involving different layers of administration on an ongoing basis and the charges reflect this. Only those Independent Financial Advisers that are suitably qualified are permitted to undertake this kind of activity, they tend to be those most highly qualified and will therefore be towards the peak of the fee scale.

Typically the initial charge will be 1%-4% of your total fund value depending upon the size of your fund. For example, if your Pension fund is £200,000 you could lose £8,000 in fees on day one.

Additionally there will be annual administration payments to the provider which could be £1,000, plus annual management of your funds, normally 1%-2% per annum and possibly payment to your Financial Adviser so be under no illusion that QROPS are cheap.

QROPS can receive transfer values from any UK registered Pension scheme (other than Annuities and with some QROPS, occupational Pensions) even where benefits are being taken. Wherever your Pension fund is currently located it will almost certainly be incurring charges in some form and it is a case of sitting down to determine if the tax advantages and increased flexibility outweigh the additional costs and this is of course something that will vary for every individual.

So is it worth it?

The trustees of your QROPS are required as part of their HMRC approval to notify them of any payment of Pensions made to you so that your liability to income tax can be calculated. However, the trustees do not have to notify HMRC if the Pension scheme member (that's you!) is not resident in the UK when the payment is made and has not been so resident for 5 tax years preceding the tax year in which the payment is made (paragraph 2 Schedule 34 Finance Act 2004). As a result no income tax will be imposed on payments from the scheme.

Put simply, the trustees of the QROPS will not have to report to HMRC any payments made to you, providing you are not tax resident in the UK in the tax year when the payment is made and have not been UK resident for tax purposes any of the previous tax 5 years. So providing it's been at least 5 years since you waved goodbye to Blighty, HMRC will not even be aware of any Pension payments made to you, nor be able to tax you upon them.

If the QROPS provider is in a country where payments from such schemes are not taxable then payments can be made to you without deduction of tax, although you may be liable to tax on the income depending on your country of residence at the time of receipt.

More tax-free cash?

If your UK Pension is transferred to a QROPS you may be able take a larger portion of your Pension`s value as a tax-free lump sum than if it had remained in the UK, but this is an area of contention and anyone promising significant amounts of tax-free loot above 25% should be approached with caution.

These so-called 'Pension liberation' schemes offering this facility are very likely to fall foul of HMRC and cause problems for you in the future. You may be able to undertake a further transfer and after 5 years of non-UK residency there are fewer restrictions. Although I certainly wouldn't recommend transferring to a QROPS with all the associated expenses purely on the possibility that you will be able to access your entire Pension fund as a tax-free lump sum some point down the line because you may well be disappointed.

More freedom

After you have been overseas for at least 5 tax years, the QROPS Pension fund becomes subject only to the laws of the relevant overseas jurisdiction in which it is based, and the requirement to commence taking benefits by a certain age no longer applies. There is no limit to the size of funds that may be invested within a QROPS and, unlike in the UK, there is no limit to the size of funds that may be accumulated within a QROPS. You therefore escape the Annual Allowance, Lifetime Allowance and any associated tax charges.

The investment choice will normally be extremely wide; you can manage the assets yourself with total freedom or work with an investment manager or Financial Adviser. After you have been a non-UK resident for 5 years the investment range is virtually unlimited. It really depends what you are looking to achieve and how involved you would like to be with the investment decisions as to your choice of investment strategy.

Assuming you have not been resident in the UK for the 5 preceding years, there are no particular limits on the amount of Pension that can be taken. There is no obligation to buy an Annuity and the amount of income which may be drawn from the fund is largely unrestricted. Dependent on the QROPS scheme you use there will usually be no deduction of tax at source either.

What will happen to my QROPS Pension fund upon my death?

With the better QROPS schemes, any funds remaining upon death will be paid to those nominated by you as beneficiaries in full. Dependent on your personal circumstances, significant tax planning opportunities may be possible as this will normally be paid as a lump sum without any deduction of tax.

So why doesn't everyone do it?

Your existing Pension schemes require careful scrutiny, the attraction of a tax-free income is obvious but make sure you don't sacrifice valuable benefits; you may have guaranteed benefits within your current scheme or there are certain valuable ancillary benefits, such as children's Pensions which wouldn't be available in a QROPS, or there may be personal reasons why you would be better suited to remaining in your current Pension scheme. It is important to examine all of these factors prior to making a decision.

QROPS arrangements can offer considerably more flexibility, greater income potential and more investment freedom than a UK Pension and with the correct advice tax benefits can be substantial for those planning to live outside of the UK for more than 5 years.

It's not just about Pensions, it is all the related legal matters; seek suitably qualified legal advice to ensure all of your affairs are in order and compatible with your destination country to avoid any legal disputes in the future. For example, Spanish inheritance laws may conflict with a Will drafted in the UK and most UK Trusts are not legally recognised in France so be sure everything is as it should be to protect your assets and your family before you pack your flip flops.

Cheers for QROPS

- ✓ Draw your income without liability to UK tax
- ✓ Choose when to draw and how much income or none at all
- ✓ No need to pay UK tax charges on death - leave your entire Pension fund to your loved ones tax free
- ✓ Take a tax-free lump sum in excess of 25% (possibly!)
- ✓ Maximum investment freedom
- ✓ Take income and benefits in the currency and location of your choice

Fears for QROPS

- × High-charging structures can take the shine off the tax advantages
- × Investor protection may not be as robust as in the UK
- × Limitations of off-the-shelf type products may prove a false economy
- × Dealing with individuals in unfamiliar jurisdictions
- × Currency risk – your Pension may be invested in a different currency to your country of residence
- × UK laws may change so there is no benefit in transferring offshore

15 The final hurdle

Protecting your assets for the future

I accept that many of the topics in this chapter can make for uncomfortable reading as none of us like to consider the onset of our own decrepitude and death, but the better prepared we are for all eventualities the easier it will be for us and our families to deal with when the situation arrives.

As your pace of life begins to reduce and you have ticked off almost all the goals on your retirement list, not only will your income needs change but you may well begin to reflect more on life and start to think deeply about the longer term and after you are gone. Virtually everything in this chapter can be put in place at any time and the sooner you do it the more content you will be that all of your affairs are in order. There is nothing to stop you writing a Will and establishing a Family Trust at age 40 and certainly the crossroads reached at retirement is an ideal time to review these issues to ensure plans are firmly in place.

Make a Will!

The simplest yet single most effective item of financial planning you could ever undertake, yet why do so many people choose not to make a Will? If they think that by not making a Will they will somehow cheat the reaper I am afraid they are wrong, as thousands of people die intestate every year. (If you die without having a Will in place you are deemed to have died intestate). By dying intestate your assets will be distributed in accordance with a set of rules over which you have no control whatsoever. Yes, making a Will is an expense, but a modest one and apart from the cost saving there are absolutely no advantages in not making a Will, unless of course you actually want to cause mayhem and distress after your death!

Not writing a Will is in fact is an act of extreme selfishness as you are leaving your family to sort out your affairs when they are least able to do so and it also creates a climate for confusion, disputes and unnecessary expense. From your own perspective, do you really want the Government to decide how your assets are distributed after your death? That's what happens if you die intestate.

A basic Will makes provision for gifts and legacies, ensuring your assets are distributed in line with your wishes rather than subject to the laws of intestacy. Many people believe that their assets will automatically pass to their chosen beneficiaries, but this is not necessarily the case. By making a Will you are ensuring that you, rather than the government, decide how your assets are distributed as well as nominating executors to manage your affairs and choosing guardians for your children if required.

In addition to the basic management and distribution of assets, the use of Wills and Trusts can be a very effective vehicle for reducing any liability for Inheritance Tax and ensuring assets remain in the family should the surviving partner remarry. It is particularly important if a couple are not married but have shared assets, living in the same house for example, because the surviving partner has no legal right to the use of any assets that are not jointly owned. Whatever your marital situation, a Family Trust can be established alongside your Will so that upon your death a proportion of your assets can be transferred into your Family Trust which can protect your assets from any unwanted interlopers – including possibly the taxman.

Intestacy laws

If you should die and no valid Will can be found, the Government then effectively makes a Will for you and your estate must be divided between certain people in accordance with a long list of rules which are too complex to enter into here. You can access the full list in a brochure and useful flowchart in the 'free downloads' section of www.estatemattersfinancial.co.uk.

Remember, if you are not married or in a civil partnership and you have not made a Will the laws of intestacy mean that if you live with someone they will be entitled to NOTHING from your estate unless it is jointly owned.

Real life…

Ruth and Dennis had lived together for 24 years. Ruth had been married to an abusive man before she met Dennis and despite Dennis's repeated romantic requests Ruth refused to marry again. When they decided to move into together Ruth provided the deposit for their home and Dennis took responsibility for the mortgage. Over the years they improved their home adding a garage and a conservatory and when Ruth began working from home, a substantial loft conversion.

Dennis collapsed and died very suddenly at work. He was only 52 and had never got around to making a Will.

The shock of losing Dennis was just the start for Ruth, she assumed that everything would simply pass to her, after all they had joint bank accounts and had been together nearly all their adult lives, but this is not the case under the rules of intestacy. As the house was in Dennis's sole name, his sister in New Zealand – who Ruth had never met – became the sole beneficiary of Dennis's estate so Ruth lost her life partner, her most valuable asset and was then made homeless, all because they never got around to making a Will.

Living Wills

A Living Will allows you to state in advance your views on how you want to be treated if you are no longer able to make rational decisions about your medical treatment. The Mental Capacity Act 2005 provides the legal framework for people to make very clear what actions they do or don't want to be taken on their behalf. Most controversially they allow you to make advance decisions to refuse treatment, even if this treatment could prolong your life.

Advance decisions and advance statements are the legal descriptions for different types of Living Wills. An advance decision refers to the refusal of treatment and an advance statement is any other direction you may wish to make about how you would like to be treated. Only an advance decision is legally binding, but an advance statement must be taken into account when family, carers or members of the medical profession are deciding upon a course of treatment for you.

When you are ill, you can usually discuss treatment with your doctor and then reach a decision about your care going forward. However, you may be admitted to hospital when unconscious or unable, on a temporary or permanent basis, to make your own decisions about your treatment or communicate your wishes. This may happen, for example, if you have an accident, suffer a stroke or develop dementia. To use the legal term you would 'lack mental capacity' to make an informed decision.

In such situations, doctors have a legal and ethical obligation to act in your best interests. One exception to this is if you have made an advance decision refusing treatment. If this decision is valid and applicable to the circumstances, medical professionals providing your care are duty bound to observe it even if they think it is not in your best interests.

If you are unfortunate enough to be told that you have a debilitating or terminal illness you may wish to prepare an advance decision indicating the type of treatment you would not want to receive in the future. Making an advance decision gives you peace of mind that your wishes will be carried out and you will be treated in the dignified way you want to be.

Powers of attorney

There may come a time in your dotage when you will want someone to look after your financial affairs even if you are still capable of doing so yourself. It could be because you are going into hospital for a long period, or simply because you just want some help keeping things in order. If this is the case you can choose to set up either an Ordinary or Lasting Power of Attorney. Remember the key word in this section is 'power' – power over your affairs, perhaps indefinitely. This is not something to be entered into lightly as you need to be absolutely sure that whoever you entrust with this role will perform their duties with your best interests at heart.

Ordinary Power of Attorney

An Ordinary Power of Attorney gives someone else the power to handle your financial affairs on your behalf. One key thing to remember about an Ordinary Power of Attorney is that it comes to an end if you lose the mental capacity to make decisions about your finances, so it may only be a temporary arrangement.

Lasting Power of Attorney

If you want someone to be able to continue looking after your finances if you lose mental capacity to make your own financial decisions, you should consider setting up a property and affairs Lasting Power of Attorney. This is a new power, that replaces the previous system of Enduring Powers of Attorney. One key difference with the new version is that as well as covering your financial affairs, you can set parameters to give someone else the authority to make decisions about your health and medical care if you are no longer capable of making those decisions yourself.

This last point is an immensely controversial area as medical science now has the capability to keep us alive, potentially for many years, in conditions that even 10 years ago would have not been possible. Hardly a week goes by without some news story raising questions about the moral rights and wrongs of dealing with this situation.

For many people this is an undesirable and undignified end to their lives and a growing number of people are documenting their wishes for their loved ones should this predicament arise. This is an eminently sensible approach, not only does it save your nearest and dearest from the anguish of making a very difficult decision at a very distressing time, it ensures that you remain in control of your own life right to the end.

HIS PENSION SCHEME WAS PANTS BUT HIS FUNERAL PLAN WAS SOMETHING ELSE

Long-term care tax

OK I know strictly speaking it isn't a tax, but if in my view it can be more pernicious, amounting to a 100% tax on all of your assets above a nominal threshold should you have to go into residential long-term care. It seems grossly unfair that everything you have worked for all your life can be decimated in a few short years to fund your place at a Local Authority Care Home.

The Community Care Act 1993 introduced the regime giving Local Authorities the right to sell your home to pay for your residential care. Every Government since, including the current one, have promised to reduce the unfairness of the system. None has come up with a workable solution. More than 100,000 homes are sold every year to fund care for their former owners; that means 100,000 elderly people have the stress of losing their home and are deprived of the right to pass it on to their children or leave the proceeds to a good cause. From a Government perspective if this system was stopped they would suddenly have to fund at least another £20bn a year. In the current economic climate that is never going to happen so you need to take steps to ensure your home is protected.

Long-term care charges can be £30,000 a year so it doesn't take long to exhaust even those comfortably off and some simple Trust planning can avoid all the heartache and ensure there is something to leave to your loved ones should you require residential care. Please don't disregard this issue on the premise that 'it won't happen to me', it is estimated that half of women and a third of men will require some form of long term care in their lifetime.

By establishing a Trust this pernicious tax can be avoided in the majority of cases. An Asset Protection Trust can help to protect your property and other assets from the Local Authority should you need to be admitted into residential care at some point in the future as even those with a modest amount of savings and income will be vulnerable to attack. The sooner you establish your trust the more likely it will be robust and effective; if you place your assets into Trust in the knowledge that you are going to need care in the near future this is considered a 'deliberate deprivation of assets' and will be invalid. The longer the period between establishing your Trust and entering care, the more likely it will protect your assets effectively. We work with a number of solicitors to support the growing demand for these types of Trusts, so we can point you in the right direction if need be. Also you can find volumes of useful information on this and related issues at www.ageuk.org.uk.

Equity release

Against a background of falling interest and Annuity rates and uncertain stock market returns, property can provide a dependable source of income for more and more Pensioners. Equity release is a method of freeing cash tied up in property. As many retired people are 'asset rich and cash poor' the money tied up in your bricks and mortar can be used for anything you wish or simply to provide a supplementary income in your later years. Additionally early release of equity can be also used as a method of reducing potential Inheritance Tax liabilities.

Make sure any equity release scheme that you consider is approved by SHIP (Safe Home Income Plans) so that you never run the risk of losing your home. Equity release can provide you with a cash sum, tax free, of up to 35% of your house's market value (assuming that you have no mortgage or other loan secured on it). You can spend or invest this sum as you wish and never have to pay it back or pay interest on it. When you sell your house or fall off your perch, the lender simply takes a share of the proceeds equivalent to the amount you released, plus interest.

If you undertake equity release not only is your house worth substantially less in terms of assessment for long-term care (and could even be valued at nothing at all). The cash released could be gifted away and over 7 years (during which it would be subject to Taper Relief from Inheritance Tax) it would be transferred out of your estate. In addition, the released cash could be used to set up a Trust which could increase your income and help reduce your IHT liability at the same time.

Pensions

If you die while receiving Pension benefits there may well be ongoing Pension payment to a Spouse, outstanding payments on a 5 or 10-year guarantee or a lump sum payable to your estate. Many of the scenarios on death we have covered in previous chapters and there are way too many variations to go into detail here.

If you are unsure what happens to your Pension when you die, speak to your Adviser or write to your Scheme Administrators who will be able to tell you in detail the options available to your loved ones and ensure that your Pension passes in line with your wishes.

Pension funds and avoiding Inheritance Tax

A common mistake made with Pension funds is for the Pension plan holder to nominate their Spouse or civil partner to receive their Pension lump sum on death, which is normally payable tax free. From an Inheritance Tax planning perspective, this simply aggravates the tax position when the last partner dies as the value of the Pension fund is then included within their taxable estate.

A simple solution to avoid this problem is to establish a Spousal By-pass Trust and make the Trust the nominated beneficiary of your Pension lump sum. This way the cash is available to your partner during their lifetime but remains outside of their estate for Inheritance Tax purposes. This also has the added advantage that by using the funds within the Trust your other half is effectively creating a debt to the Trust, a debt that must be repaid on their death, thereby reducing their estate for Inheritance Tax purposes even further – so a double tax whammy that works in your favour for once!

Inheritance Tax (IHT)

There are many uncomplicated ways that you can reduce any liability you may have to Inheritance Tax. Some methods can be unnecessarily complex and very often a few simple and cost-effective measures involving Wills and Trusts can solve the problem.

What exactly is Inheritance Tax?

Inheritance Tax is potentially charged on your estate when you die. It is a very simple but largely avoidable tax. A tax charge of 40% is levied on everything you possess above a financial threshold of £325,000 which is known as the Nil Rate Band (NRB).

When I say everything you own – I mean everything you own! It is charged against the net value of everything in your estate including your house, any holiday home or investment properties, cash, savings, investments including ISAs, National Savings, shares, cars, jewellery etc. Assessment will also include the value of any Pension lump sums or life assurance policies that are not in Trust.

Any percentage of the NRB which was unused when the first Spouse or civil partner dies may be transferred to the surviving partner to be used when calculating their own IHT liability when they die. This effectively makes the NRB, the threshold before any liability for Inheritance Tax is payable, £650,000 for married couples and civil partnerships.

Rises in property values in the last 10 years and increased personal wealth mean that many more people own assets which are (or will be) valued well above the NRB threshold. Without prudent IHT planning your family could be faced with a very large tax liability when you die.

One very important point to understand about Inheritance Tax is that it MUST be paid before your estate can be released to your beneficiaries. None of your assets can be used to pay the tax, the money will have to be found elsewhere by your children or nominated Executors, this is usually done in the form a of a bank loan – not a thing you really want your children to be organising at such a stressful time.

How much Inheritance Tax will my estate have to pay?

If you take no action to reduce your IHT liability and there is no unused NRB to transfer to you resulting from the death of your Spouse or civil partner, the table below provides an indication of what your IHT liability could be:

Estate Value	Amount liable to Tax	IHT payable at 40%
£300,000	£0	£0
£400,000	£75,000	£30,000
£500,000	£175,000	£70,000
£600,000	£275,000	£110,000
£700,000	£375,000	£150,000
£800,000	£475,000	£190,000
£900,000	£575,000	£230,000
£1,000,000	£675,000	£270,000

By planning appropriately and making full use of the allowances available your IHT liability can be mitigated by legitimately reducing the value of your taxable estate. It is very important to consider planning well in advance, ideally early in retirement while you are still in good health as there can be an IHT liability for up to 7 years from the date you make your arrangements.

Key IHT allowances, reliefs and exemptions

There are a range of reliefs and exemptions which can be applied to your estate that will significantly reduce your Inheritance Tax liability. Below is brief a summary of those available. You should, of course, always take professional advice on the viability of these allowances in relation to your own individual circumstances.

The Nil Rate Band (NRB) As discussed above the NRB for each individual is £325,000 which effectively gives a total Nil Rate Band per couple of £650,000. The actual amount of NRB to be transferred is calculated by assessing the proportion (as a percentage) of the NRB that was unused at the time of the first death and applying the same proportion to the current NRB available at the time of the second death.

Given that any transfer of assets between Spouses or civil partners is exempt from IHT, if a Spouse or civil partner dies and leaves all of his or her estate to the surviving Spouse or partner, the NRB threshold for the survivor would be double the then current individual NRB level.

Gifting of assets and associated exemptions Gifts to certain beneficiaries are not subject to IHT. Others are subject to IHT but the rate of Tax reduces to zero over a period of 7 years.

Gifts (or Transfers of Assets as they are termed) to the following beneficiaries are exempt from IHT:

- Spouse/civil partner
- Registered charities
- Political parties
- Institutions for national purposes (for example the National Trust)

Additional IHT exemptions include:

Annual Exemptions Individuals can give away up to £3,000 per tax year.

Small Gift Exemptions Gifts of up to £250 can be made to any number of individuals.

Normal Expenditure Exemption - gifts that are considered to be made from income. These Gifts must be made regularly (say annually or monthly) and must come from after-tax income.

Marriage or Civil Partnership Exemption Gifts made by certain individuals in the case of a wedding or civil partnership for example parents can gift up to £5,000.

Usually the majority of gifts that do not fall into the above categories, including settlements into certain types of Trust are considered Potentially Exempt Transfers.

15.10 Potentially Exempt Transfers These are commonly known to as PETs although they do not require feeding or unwanted trips to the vets. The IHT rate applicable to PETs depends upon the number of years that have passed between the date the gift was made and the death of the benefactor. The rate of tax to be paid is on a sliding scale reducing over 7 years to zero. The rates of tax applied are as follows:

Years between gift and death	Reduction in tax rate
0-3	0%
3-4	20%
4-5	40%
5-6	60%
6-7	80%
7	100%

Simple ways to reduce Inheritance Tax using investments and Trusts

Among the many ways of mitigating your IHT liability, here are two simple, quick and inexpensive options using existing investments with Trusts:

1. Discounted Gift Trusts
2. Gift and Loan Trusts

Discounted Gift Trusts (DGT)

These are a method of reducing IHT suitable for both single people and couples. How it works is that you decide upon the amount you wish to invest and the level of income that you require (this is normally 5% for maximum tax benefits). A calculation is then undertaken based upon your age and state of health at commencement with assumptions made about your life expectancy to determine the level of the discount, which is ultimately determined by HMRC. As you are taking an income, this amount, calculated with your estimated life expectancy, is discounted from your capital for IHT purposes.

Below is a *rough* guide to the level of discount you could receive:

	Male	Female
Age 60	60%	67%
Age 70	54%	55%
Age 80	32%	40%

For example, if you are a 70-year-old woman and you invest £100,000 in an investment held within a Discounted Gift Trust, you can take £5,000 a year as income and have £55,000 outside of your estate immediately reducing your IHT bill by £22,000, with the remaining £45,000 falling outside your estate completely after 7 years, reducing your potential IHT bill by a further £18,000.

By placing an investment in such a Trust the potential advantages are:

- An immediate reduction in the Inheritance Tax liability on your estate
- A further tax saving after 7 years
- Capital for your family or chosen beneficiaries after your death
- Tax-efficient regular payments during your lifetime
- You choose your payment level and its frequency
- A choice of investment Bonds
- Diverse investments within the Bonds, helping to spread your risk
- All investment growth is outside of your estate
- Single or joint arrangements

Joyce is 60 years old and places her £100,000 investment Bond within a DGT. What are the tax consequences?

	Without a Discounted Gift Trust	**With a Discounted Gift Trust**
Original investment	£100,000	£100,000
Discount applicable	n/a	£67,000
Amount potentially liable to IHT	£100,000	£33,000
Maximum amount of IHT during first 7 years	£40,000	£13,200
Maximum amount of IHT after 7 years	£40,000	£0

Real life…

For example: Mr Khan invests £100,000 in a Discounted Gift Trust. Mr Khan is 60 years old and in good health. He chooses to withdraw £5,000 per annum from the plan to supplement his Pension income. His investment immediately receives a discount for tax purposes of £60,000, which means that this amount is no longer liable to Inheritance Tax.

The remaining £40,000 is treated as a Potentially Exempt Transfer (PET) and will be subject to IHT Taper Relief. If Mr Khan survives 7 years, all of his initial £100,000 will become totally exempt from Inheritance Tax as is all the growth on his investment. Plus, of course, he can continue to benefit from a tax-efficient income.

Gift and Loan Trusts (GLT)

These are particularly suitable for individuals who want to retain access to their original capital but use the scheme as a vehicle to avoid paying increasing Inheritance Tax on the growth of their capital over time. With this type of scheme, all growth on the original capital takes place outside of the individual's estate for the purposes of Inheritance Tax.

Loan schemes work in the following way:

a. Establish a Discretionary Trust and loan the Trust an amount of capital
b. The Trust invests the original capital to produce growth
c. Under the Trust rules you have the right for the capital to be paid back to you partially or in full at anytime in the form of an interest-free loan
d. You withdraw money from the Trust in the form of a loan as and when required to supplement your income or for capital expenditure
e. Upon your death your estate must repay the loan in full, this is considered a debt upon your estate and therefore reduces the value of your estate for IHT purposes

Any amount of the original capital loan not repaid at the time of death (for example, you did not 'borrow' the full amount that you originally placed in the Trust) will form part of your estate for IHT purposes, but any capital growth the Trust may have enjoyed will remain outside of your estate.

Inheritance Tax – during your lifetime

There will be an immediate tax charge if the value of any Gifts you make, together with any other chargeable transfers you have made in the previous 7 years, are more than the Nil Rate Band (£325,000). An example of a chargeable transfer would be a Gift into a Discretionary Trust although if you are setting up the Trust as a couple, you will each have your own Nil Rate Band. The immediate tax charge is 20% of the amount above the Nil Rate Band that you gift.

There may also be a periodic charge on Trusts every 10 years. This will be a maximum of 6% of the value of the Trust fund, but is likely to be less in many cases. If the Trust fund is worth less than the Nil Rate Band at that time, and you hadn't made any other chargeable transfers in the seven years before setting up your Trust, the periodic charge will be zero. Both the immediate and the periodic charges will be based on the discounted value of the Trust. Where two people set up the Trust, the charges will be assessed individually, based on each person's discounted gift and Nil Rate Band. The value of the Trust fund is not included within the estates of your beneficiaries.

Inheritance Tax – exit charges

When money is paid out of the Trust to your beneficiaries, either while you are alive or after your death, there may be an exit charge. This is based on the previous periodic charge (or the charge when the Trust was set up, if there hasn't yet been a 10-year periodic charge), but takes into account the Nil Rate Band at the time. If the previous charge was nil, the exit charge will also be nil, even if the value of the Trust fund has grown. Where there is an exit charge, the maximum rate that will apply is currently 6% although fortunately any regular payments are not subject to any exit charge.

Life assurance to beat Inheritance Tax

Life assurance policies can be used to help with Inheritance Tax planning. Policies are written in Trust, so that on death the sum assured is paid into the Trust and does not form part of your estate.

Be aware that if you have any existing life assurance policies that are not written in Trust the sum payable will form part of your estate and could be liable for Inheritance Tax.

Using life assurance in this way ensures that your family has available capital to hand to pay the IHT which may arise in the event of your death without having to arrange a loan or use their own funds; remember none of your assets can be sold to pay IHT. The tax must be paid to the Revenue before the assets from your estate are released to your beneficiaries and an appropriate life assurance policy can provide the funding for this.

Whole of Life insurance policies

As I am sure you can ascertain, a Whole of Life is just that, it provides life assurance cover for the whole of your life and will pay out even if you live to be 120 years old!

They can be taken out for an individual or as a joint plan to cover two people, typically a Spouse or civil partner. A joint plan usually provides cover on a 'joint life second death' basis where no payment is made upon the death of the first person insured but full payment is made upon the death of the second party – usually to pay off any IHT liability.

As the proceeds of this type of cover are normally designed to pay off some or all of the final IHT liability, the level of cover is often set at an estimate of what your eventual IHT liability is likely to be. Payment of the sum assured would be made into a suitable Trust on the second death so that it would not form part of the estate. You do, of course, have the cost of paying the premiums (why not get the kids to pay them – after all they are going to benefit!). This can be a more cost-effective option than giving up access to capital or the future growth of that capital, or you may simply not want or be in a position to gift assets away at this time.

As with all assets that are placed in Trust there are two additional advantages:

The Trust assets can be paid out immediately on death, they are not subject to the lengthy probate process which can take 6 months or more, thereby placing the Trust assets in the hands of your chosen beneficiaries without delay.

Furthermore, unlike the provisions of your Will, the terms of the Trust cannot be contested after your death, so you are assured of your wishes being carried out without legal challenge.

Legacies: Your gifts to the world

An increasing number of people want to feel their lives have been for some purpose greater than what they see around them and wish to leave the world a better place than they found it by arranging to leave a monetary gift to their favourite charity. There are a number of tax-efficient ways to achieve this and many of the larger well-known charities such as the RSPCA are largely funded by legacies.

These generous people make a huge difference to the world and we have developed a method of making their generosity spread even further. You can now make an even greater difference at no additional cost and take steps to ensure that the funds are in place prior to your passing. For full information please visit our website www.legacynetwork.co.uk but below is a brief outline of how the system works – this is an unashamed plug for our charity work!

So how does it work?

You decide which charities you would like to bequeath a Gift and how much you would like that Gift to be. We then estimate what that amount could be turned into if you are to pay it monthly for the rest of your life or if you wish to leave a lump sum in your Will.

Monthly contributions

You could decide that you wish to leave a specific amount to charity, regardless of when you die. For example, Mr & Mrs Generous, a 65 year old couple decide to donate £100,000 to their chosen charity. This can be achieved by paying £175 per month into a Life Assurance Legacy Policy, so that your charity is guaranteed to receive £100,000 when the last of Mr & Mrs Generous passes away, providing they continue to pay the premiums and the policy is placed in an appropriate Trust for the charity (we can arrange this for you).

Lump sum legacy

You have a lump sum you are planning to leave to your chosen charity which you invest in a tax-efficient investment and use some of your return to fund the monthly premium for your legacy policy. For example, using our 65-year-old couple, above, their legacy policy for £100,000 would cost them £175 per month. If they invest their £100,000, even a return of 4% per annum would be more than sufficient to pay for their legacy policy premiums and provide a hedge against inflation. This method has three distinct advantages;

1. You retain the use of your capital to draw on if you should need it
2. You don't have to worry about paying the premiums to fund your legacy policy; this will be taken care of automatically by your investment
3. The invested capital (plus any growth) can also be left to your chosen charity if you so wish, thereby doubling the size of your Gift or it can be left to another beneficiary

So what's the benefit?

In our example of Mr & Mrs Generous wishing to leave £100,000, if both were to live for 20 years to age 85 the legacy policy would have cost them £42,000 (£175 x 12 months x 20 years) but their chosen charity still benefits by £100,000.

Does it always work out better value than simply leaving an amount in my Will?

It certainly should do. Using our example of Mr and Mrs Generous who started their legacy policy at age 65, one of them would have to live to be 112 years old to be worse off and whilst I am not saying it couldn't happen...

This has five added advantages:

1. Your legacy to charity is guaranteed
2. The amount you leave to charity can be far greater than you originally planned
3. You can use the residue of your capital for living expenses
4. The capital can be invested to fund your monthly premiums
5. Your premiums reduce your estate for IHT purposes

This is never an exact science as none of us know how long we are going to be here but it is highly unlikely you will be worse off, although, of course the costs of your policy are determined by your age and state of health at outset.

Whatever your age or the amount of legacy you would like to leave there is a more than fighting chance we can vastly increase the amount bequeathed to your chosen charity at no extra cost to you.

Conclusion

Basic Wills and Trust planning can take care of the majority of your needs and ensure your home and other assets are protected for you and eventually for your family. Inheritance Tax is often described as a voluntary tax and one that can largely be avoided. The best way to deal with the problem will depend upon your own particular circumstances and appropriate planning can only be arrived at by careful consideration of your own individual situation. This can only really be achieved by sitting down with a professional Adviser considering all of the options and then compiling a list of recommendations that will work best for you. Very often these do not have to be particularly complex or expensive.

I appreciate there is a lot to absorb in this chapter but I know from experience with clients there is both a sense of relief and fulfilment when their estate protection strategies are put in place. Unfortunately, the scenarios we are considering are all rather grim but they are all potential scenarios that we will all have to face at some point and I believe they will be easier to face with the peace of mind that all of our affairs are in order and that our loved ones are looked after as tax efficiently and effectively as possible.

16 The call to arms

Everyone needs a plan. What's yours?

"I hope I die before I get old," screamed Roger Daltrey and we all sang along in agreement. It would never happen to us, it was a million light years away and 'old' was for that uncool alien generation that went before us with their outdated attitudes and strange views. From where we were standing that refusal to grow up and live lives like our parents was, in some bizarre way, a force for good yet the 'No future' Johnny Rotten snarled about turned up anyway, regardless of his threats.

It all happened so fast, there we were having a good time, our only concern was where the next £5 was coming from so we could go out on a Friday night or buy the latest record (remember records?) and before we even had time to really think, never mind start saving properly, here we are having to make decisions about our Pensions and plan our retirement.

Well, Mr Daltrey, things have changed, and you should know because you're a Pensioner too. I hope I get old before I die and I hope I have enough money to enjoy it. It is impossible to define what being 'old' means anymore and in a strange form of belated youthful rebellion Pensioners are refusing to fit quietly into their allotted stereotypes that society has defined for them.

In the same way we can no longer define retirement as easily as we did even 20 years ago, everything has become blurred, retirement has become a very personal journey and increasingly one that we can design ourselves. To do that we are faced with the tyranny of choice, of making lifetime decisions on a subject about which there is an unlimited amount of information, but very little actual help and advice.

Whether you have a vocation, a career, a calling, or just a job and no matter whether you skip down the path every morning or consider every day another day to be survived in the Gulag, you will reach a point where either you or some external force decides it is time to start slowing down or even step off the hamster wheel completely. When that day comes, you want to be in a position to face it with confidence, secure in the knowledge that you are on the right road and not starting your personal journey into the heart of retirement darkness.

Your retirement, like mine, will arrive with a unique set of circumstances that requires a unique set of solutions. Very few people that come to me arrive at their retirement on the terms that they had envisaged perhaps only 10 years before, rarely do people feel they have enough money and I am yet to meet anyone who feels they have too much. The majority feel they face an uncertain future; even those with adequate financial provision face critical choices that will affect the rest of their lives and are unsure how to evaluate those choices, never mind actually reach a decision.

There are certain aspects that all retirements have in common and now you have read this book you know what to do:

1. Clarify your priorities – take a weekend, at least, to sort out your life and decide what you really want out of retirement, what your financial needs are, and most importantly your goals.

2. Decide if you are going to do everything yourself or, if selecting an Adviser, what you want out of the relationship

3. Decide upon an investment and income strategy

4. Make a Will or review your existing Will, consider establishing Trusts, protect your home AND think about legacies at www.legacynetwork.co.uk

5. Review your financial strategy at least annually

6. Enjoy your retirement!

If you are still saving for retirement ask yourself: "How much will I really need in £'s before I have got too much money?" And if you have not reached that figure yet – keep saving!

No Pension income method is necessarily better than another and no one investment strategy superior to that of its peers, but used in combination and the right proportion they can provide you with the optimum remedy to your retirement income dilemma.

As we know there is a lot of star gazing required in planning your retirement income but careful and considered planning at outset will help reduce the chances of your retirement plans ending up in a black hole. All the options described in his book are planets in your retirement universe and those planets may come into alignment in a different sequence and at different times to create the most harmonious solution to your retirement needs.

I hope this book has gone some way to providing you with the guidance you need to take those first hesitant steps into the retirement light and towards making those lifetime decisions with renewed confidence. Of course, I have had the benefit of experiencing hundreds of retirements at close quarters and while everyone's retirement plan will be as unique as a snowflake there are common elements that will apply regardless of who you are, where you live or how much money you have got. Remember it's the quality of life not the quantity of loot that will determine how happy your retirement turns out to be.

We are living in truly ground breaking times, never have there been more opportunities for those approaching retirement, the choices we have are almost limitless. Ironically our desires and expectations are equally as limitless and you are being presented with a singular chance to explore yourself and the wider world. We are healthier and wealthier than we have ever been at any time in human history and the quality and quantity of life is being continually extended beyond boundaries that even 50 years ago appeared impossible.

For the first time people are spending more time in retirement than they did at work and this brings with it not only opportunity but challenge, perhaps the most significant of which is how to fund and budget for the next 20, 30, 40 or may be even 50 years. Don't be retiring in your retirement, having the right financial plan and investment strategy in place will almost certainly make that long journey both less arduous and more interesting. I hope this book has gone some way towards lifting the fog and providing you with some clarity of vision as to the realistic options available to you and your hard-earned funds.

You may not end up with the retirement you dreamed of but at least you will, with any luck, end up with the retirement you have chosen. If you want more information you can always look us up at www.pensionmatters.net and remember the wise words of Seneca contemplating retirement to the Roman countryside 2,000 years ago: "Life is only short and anxious for those who forget the past, neglect the present and fear the future" so make sure you go out there and enjoy it to the full.

The End

About the Author

Paul Steel is a Chartered and ISO Certified Financial Planner, a Pensions enthusiast who has been advising clients on retirement planning for more than 20 years. Paul is also an elected Fellow of the Chartered Insurance Institute, a Fellow of the Personal Finance Society, and a qualifying member of the Million Dollar Round Table, the premier worldwide organisation for financial services professionals.

Paul's day job as a retirement planning specialist involves helping clients make key financial decisions at significant milestones in their lives, offering guidance and support both before and after that pivotal retirement date. He is currently employed as an Adviser and Director of Estate Matters Financial Limited, an investment and Pensions boutique based in Gateshead in the North East of England.

Lightning Source UK Ltd.
Milton Keynes UK
21 February 2011

167957UK00001B/54/P